Bible Study Guide

A One-Year Beginner's
Chronological
Guide to the Bible
(66 Books)

Anders Bennett

The Bible is a collection of ancient writings about God and His plan to save His people. These writings were penned over 1,500 years by around 40 authors, using 3 languages, and consist of 66 books. The Bible itself claims to be the Word of God (2 Timothy 3:16-17). It tells us that its authors were inspired by God as they wrote (2 Peter 1:21). The amazing thing about the Bible is that all these different sources over such a great span of time all tell the same story. It is a story called the Gospel or the good news.

As you read the Bible, you will see these Gospel themes highlighted on every page: themes that include grace, forgiveness, and mercy; themes that accept justice, holiness, and righteousness. These Gospel themes and stories center around Jesus. The entire first half of the Bible, called the Old Testament, points its readers to look for Jesus. He will be called a coming Prophet, Priest, and King. The second half of the Bible, called the New Testament, tells the story of Jesus' coming, His life, death, and resurrection, and explains how His sacrifice is good news for all who would believe.

You can summarize the entire Bible with one famous verse, John 3:16, which says, "For God so loved the world, that he gave his only Son, that whoever believes in him should not perish but have eternal life." I'm excited for you as you begin this journey. There will be sections that will be hard to understand. I want to encourage you to press on. It takes a lifetime to understand God's Word. But I promise you, every step of the journey is satisfying and joyful.

This Bible reading guide is a chronological one. That means that you will be reading each of the passages of Scripture as close to the order that they were written as we know. Many books of the Bible were written around the same time and recorded the same events from different perspectives. In order to read them in chronological order, you'll have to "jump around" in the Bible from time to time. Ultimately, this will help you keep the overarching story in order as you read.

Each week, you will have different sections of Scripture to read with a brief explanation of them. As you encounter new books, you will have an overview of the book to help you understand the big picture before you read all of the details. These resources are there to make reading this vast book more manageable and understandable. At the end of each week, you will have some questions to help you reflect and remember the information that you've encountered.

One more thing to keep in mind that this book cannot offer is the value of community. If you find yourself struggling to understand something in the Bible, reach out to a friend and work on it together. As you will see, a faith community is vital to the health of any believer. Are you ready to begin the most important spiritual journey of your life? Are you prepared to encounter God through His Word? Come with me as we begin in the beginning when God created the heavens and the earth.

Genesis

AUTHOR

Moses

GENRE

Historical Narrative

PURPOSE

Genesis tells us all of the beginnings. It tells us that there was no beginning with God. He is eternal and everlasting. It tells us the beginning of all creation. It, sadly, tells us the beginning of sin and separation from God. And wonderfully, it tells us the beginning of our salvation.

This foundational book starts with Adam and Eve, the first created human beings. The story of their fall, and the subsequent fall of humanity, will break your heart. However, the compassion of God should begin to heal it. Although they are removed from the Garden, He is sure to clothe them. He then begins working in the cosmic background to put everything in place to bring about redemption.

The key character in this book is Abraham. God is going to make a covenant with Abraham that sets him apart as God's chosen person, who will be the father of His people. It is through this covenant community that God will send His Son, Jesus, to save the world. This is where it all begins.

KEY VERSE

Genesis 12:1-3

AUTHOR

Unknown

It is unlikely that Job himself wrote this book. Traditionally, the author would name himself in a book like this. Most scholars would claim that Moses or Solomon are the authors. Some suggest Abraham, considering that Job was his contemporary.

GENRE

Wisdom Literature

PURPOSE

Ever since Genesis 3, there has been suffering in this world due to sin. The purpose of the Book of Job is to wrestle with the questions that come with suffering. Job endures tragedy after tragedy and finds himself in great physical and emotional pain before the book can really get started. If anyone has a right to lash out in anger over the suffering he has experienced, it would be him.

However, throughout his interactions with his family and friends, he remains faithful to God. And when he reaches his breaking point and calls out to God, He graciously answers Job. I'll let you read His sobering answer to the problem of suffering as you finish the book for yourself.

KEY VERSE

Job 1:20-21

On the Beginning

SCRIPTURE READINGS

Day One: **Genesis 1-3**
Day Two: **Genesis 4-7**
Day Three: **Genesis 8-11**
Day Four: **Job 1-5**
Day Five: **Job 6-9**
Day Six: **Job 10-13**
Day Seven: **Job 14-16**

SUMMARIES

Day One: **Genesis 1-3**

These chapters contain the story of creation and its corruption. It is beautiful and tragic. As you read, pay close attention to Chapter 3, verse 15. There, you will find the first promise of redemption for God's people through Jesus. It is a promise that takes a few thousand years to be fulfilled, but nevertheless, God is faithful to keep His word.

Day Two: **Genesis 4-7**

The problem of sin rears its ugly head quickly in the life of Adam and Eve. Their son commits the first murder in history. As humanity spreads, so does the sin nature they have inherited from Adam. The wickedness grows so unbearable that God wipes the slate clean and starts over with Noah and his family.

Day Three: **Genesis 8-11**

As the floodwaters subside, Noah and his family start life again. They worship the Lord, and He promises never to destroy the earth in that way again. However, the season of worship is short-lived. Humanity is fruitful and multiplies, but they refuse to cover the earth. Instead, they huddle in one city and try to make a name for themselves. God punishes them and forces them to spread out.

Day Four: **Job 1-5**

The book of Job takes place chronologically around the same time as Genesis 11-12. This book will give you a different perspective of how God is working alongside the "main plot" of the Bible. In comparison to the Garden of Eden, Satan will be at work trying to tempt God's people away from Him.

Day Five: **Job 6-9**

In these chapters, Job gets counsel from his friends as he tries to understand his desperate state. His friends, however, misunderstand the situation. They blame Job for things that we know are not true. This drives Job to despair, and he cries out to God for relief and understanding.

Day Six: **Job 10-13**

Job's friends do not relent in their counsel to him. They continue to offer up their reasonings for Job's pain. Everything from Job's own sin to Job's deserving of this helpless state is proclaimed by them. Amazingly enough, while this shakes Job's faith, it does not destroy it. A hint of hope is seen in these chapters.

Day Seven: **Job 14-16**

Job begins to be fed up with this conversation he is having with his friends. He ends up calling them miserable comforters. What started out as genuine concern from his friends seems to have turned into a theological game. In the fun of trying to pinpoint the reason for his pain, they have stopped trying to be there for him in this difficult season.

1. What does it tell you about God that in the midst of His curse of Adam, Eve, and the serpent, He includes a promise of redemption?

2. Why is holiness such an important part of God's people?

3. What makes obedience a life-or-death decision for God's people?

4. When your friends are struggling, how can you respond to their pain?

5. When you're going through a difficult time, what can you do to remind yourself of God's plan?

6. What advice would you give to Job?

7. What hope is there for the believer when their world falls apart?

SCRIPTURE READINGS

Day One: **Job 17-20**
Day Two: **Job 21-23**
Day Three: **Job 24-28**
Day Four: **Job 29-31**
Day Five: **Job 32-34**
Day Six: **Job 35-37**
Day Seven: **Job 38-39**
Day Seven: **Job 40-42**

SUMMARIES

Day One: **Job 17-20**

The faith of Job comes shining through in the midst of the increased accusations from his friends. Where they would blame Job and say that what he has endured is clearly the punishment of God, Job has a different outlook. He cannot understand the why, but he knows the who: His Redeemer. That is where his hope comes from.

Day Two: **Job 21-23**

The steadfast faith of Job seems to have gained a crack in these chapters. His friends continue to point the finger at him, and Job replies, "Where is God?" The great Redeemer in whom he has placed his trust is silent. Job wrestles with questions we all do in these next chapters.

Day Three: **Job 24-28**

As you read, you're nearing the end of Job's interactions with his friends. There seemed to be a crack forming in his faith, be it sealed tightly as Job settled in. He makes statements like, "I will maintain my integrity" and "God's majesty is unsearchable." It is difficult to imagine all that he has endured. To see the faith that remains can be inspiring.

Job 29-31

In these chapters, you will read Job's final remarks to his friends. He has had enough of this conversation. He has taken all of the verbal punishment that he can. There has been no comfort in their words. Now, he rests his case, and he places his whole trust in God's sovereign plan in it all.

Day Five: Job 32-34

Job's friend, Elihu, takes center stage for the next few sections of Scripture. At first, he rebukes the other friends of Job for their lack of care. You'll be ready to cheer him on. But not too fast. He turns towards Job and rebukes him as well. He claims the justice of God in the midst of it all and repeats much of what Job's other friends have said.

Day Six: Job 35-37

Elihu is about to take a bow as he ends his discourse on God's justice. Sadly, Elihu doesn't know what we know: that this all happened to Job to show his faithfulness to God. This didn't take place to reveal his lack of character. Elihu proclaims a lot of wonderful truth but misses the mark on how it is being applied in Job's life.

Day Seven: Job 38-39

Finally, the moment has come that Job and his friends have been begging for. After hours and days of discourse between Job and his friends about God's will, now it is revealed. God Himself answers Job. However, His answer is not what Job or his friends were hoping for. They weren't given the back story of Chapter 1 like we were.

1. Who do you know that has extraordinary faith like Job?

2. What have you endured that has tested your faith?

3. What is the significance of how God answers Job?

4. What did Elihu get right about the situation?

5. What did Elihu get wrong?

6. When have you judged a situation wrongly?

7. How can you keep from misjudging a person's circumstances?

The Answer of God

SCRIPTURE READINGS

Day One: **Job 40-42**
Day Two: **Genesis 12-15**
Day Three: **Genesis 16-18**
Day Four: **Genesis 19-21**
Day Five: **Genesis 22-24**
Day Six: **Genesis 25-26**
Day Seven: **Genesis 27-29**

SUMMARIES

Day One: **Job 40-42**

The conclusion to the Book of Job does not answer every question, but it does put them all into perspective. It causes the reader to consider the question, "Who am I to question the ways of God?" After this gut-wrenching, heart-breaking trial and proof of Job's faith, a wonderful reward is provided.

Day Two: **Genesis 12-15**

And we're back! The story of Job takes place during the life of Abraham, who is introduced in these chapters. Seemingly out of nowhere comes this man who is chosen by God to be the father of the people of God. These chapters contain one of the most important sections of Scripture in all of the Bible. God's covenant with Abraham will carry weight all the way to the New Testament.

Day Three: **Genesis 16-18**

The tragic irony of God's promise to make Abraham into a father of nations is that Abraham's wife, Sarai, is pregnant. This painful reality will color her view of the covenant and tempt them to make plans of their own. While God makes them wait a significant amount of time, He will be faithful to His promises.

Day Four: **Genesis 19-21**

Abraham is making a name for himself. His family is growing in prosperity and influence in this new land God has led them towards. He has proven himself as a military leader and a faithful family member. He has gained the attention of the watching world, and the stage is set for God to make his name great as he promised.

Day Five: **Genesis 22-24**

In these chapters, there is a great promise fulfilled and a transition that happens. God keeps His promise and provides Abraham with a son, Isaac. This son is not only a treasure to Abraham because he is a father. This son also represents a lineage that will see all of the promises of God come to fruition. Because of Isaac's birth, God can provide Abraham's family with a people, a place, and protection for generations to come.

Day Six: **Genesis 25-26**

Isaac and his wife faced many of the same difficulties as Abraham and Sarah. Consequently, they saw many of the same provisions of God in their life. It is clear to the reader that the same God is keeping the same covenant with the same family. The descendants of Abraham are explained, but the lineage through Isaac is focused on. The one who will be called Israel (the name given to the nation) is on his way.

The main character and one who receives the continued covenant promises of God is none other than the trickster, Jacob. Jacob gets a dose of his own medicine as he is tricked by his uncle, Laban. It is becoming clear that while these are God's chosen people, they are not perfect. God uses these sinful people to keep His promises.

1. Are you satisfied with God's final answer and blessing of Job? Why or why not?

2. What does God's choosing of Abraham teach you about God?

3. Have you ever faced a long season of waiting on God like Abraham and Sarah?

4. What is the significance (if any) of the barrenness issue from one generation to the next?

5. How do you feel about God's use of sinful people in His plan?

6. What type of person would you have chosen if you were to start a new nation?

7. What character trait of God is shown in His blessing of Leah?

All Things for Good

SCRIPTURE READINGS

Day One: **Genesis 30-31**

Day Two: **Genesis 32-34**

Day Three: **Genesis 35-37**

Day Four: **Genesis 38-40**

Day Five: **Genesis 41-42**

Day Six: **Genesis 43-45**

Day Seven: **Genesis 46-47**

SUMMARIES

Day One: **Genesis 30-31**

God has blessed Jacob tremendously as He did his father and grandfather. With all that he needs and wants in hand, he flees back to the Promised Land of God to continue what Abraham had started. Jacob seems to have become a different person after his dealings with Laban and his marriage to Rachel.

Day Two: **Genesis 32-34**

The confident trickster now becomes the fearful runner. Jacob realizes that he should not get away with all that he has done. Sooner rather than later, he will have to face his brother Esau. However, it is not Esau who wrestles with Jacob, but God. God gives Jacob a reminder of His presence and blessing in His life during the sparring session.

Day Three: **Genesis 35-37**

Another pivotal moment has arrived in the story of God's people. Jacob is renamed as Israel by God. Jacob then has twelve sons from his two wives. All of these names will be reflected in the nation to come. The people of God by Abraham's lineage will be called Israel, and they will settle into one nation divided into twelve tribes, reflecting the names of the twelve sons. The blueprint for God's people is in place.

Day Four: **Genesis 38-40**

Although the story is interrupted by Judah's sin with Tamar, the main character and recipient of the blessing of God is Joseph. In fact, we read more about Joseph than any other character in Genesis, except Abraham himself. The reason so much attention is given to Joseph is because his story explains how Israel left the Promised Land and ended up as slaves to Egypt.

Day Five: **Genesis 41-42**

Joseph is treated terribly by his brothers, falsely accused by Potiphar's wife, and forgotten by the prisoners he helped. With Job-like sorrow, Joseph spends much of his life in chains and bondage. The sorrow is not the only echo heard. Job-like faith resounds as Joseph remains in full trust of God's plan. Little did he expect, he would come face to face with his brothers who betrayed him.

Day Six: **Genesis 43-45**

Joseph must have been shocked to see most of his brothers actually bowing before him as the dream had revealed. The interesting twist is that Joseph recognized them but did not recognize him. How would they, after so many years away from him? He now resided and looked like an Egyptian while they still looked like his family always had. Joseph uses different tactics to find out all he can about his brothers to see if they have changed at all.

Day Seven: **Genesis 46-47**

What a reversal of power in these final chapters of Joseph's recorded life. The one who was in the pit as his brothers towered over, now held his family's fate in his hands. Joseph's godly character comes shining through as the story comes to a close. He does not punish but provides for his family. He sees how God has used, even the betrayal of his brother, to deliver a greater good.

1. Why do you think we read about such a large shift in Jacob's conduct?

____

____

2. How does Jacob's blessing from God reflect the covenant originally given to Abraham?

____

____

3. Do you think there is significance in the name Israel?

____

____

4. Why do you think so much of Genesis is focused on Joseph?

____

____

5. How would you respond to your brothers if they had betrayed you?

____

____

6. What does this teach you about forgiveness and mercy?

____

____

7. How do the lessons of Job help you to understand the life of Joseph?

____

____

Exodus

AUTHOR

Moses

GENRE

Historical Narrative

PURPOSE:

The Book of Exodus is about the great exodus of God's people from Egypt. Genesis comes to a close; God's people are living on the outskirts of Egypt due to a famine that has decimated the land. This temporary relocation turned into their permanent home over a few hundred years. Sadly, they went from free citizens of the area to slaves through a new regime.

The new Pharaoh of Egypt had no respect for the Israelites or their God. When he sees the population grow, he institutes various rules and regulations designed to threaten God's people. However, the Lord causes them to flourish and ultimately delivers them from the hands of the wicked Pharoah.

The majority of the Book of Exodus describes the journey through the wilderness as God leads them out of slavery towards the promised land. Through that journey, God renews the covenant He made with Abraham and brings more structure to it through Moses. The core of the promises has not changed, but how God's people are to live in light of the promises is made clear through the Law.

KEY VERSE

Exodus 29:46

SCRIPTURE READINGS

Day One: **Genesis 48-50**
Day Two: **Exodus 1-3**
Day Three: **Exodus 4-6**
Day Four: **Exodus 7-9**
Day Five: **Exodus 10-12**
Day Six: **Exodus 13-15**
Day Seven: **Exodus 16-18**

SUMMARIES

Day One: **Genesis 48-50**

It is a beautiful ending to a story of tragedy and intrigue. The family reunion between father and son is a fitting way to draw to a close the book of Genesis. The stage is now set for God's people to be saved under the leadership of Joseph in Egypt. Sadly, these hands that provide for Israel and his family will turn to capture them. As Genesis closes, Exodus picks up the story in chains.

Day Two: **Exodus 1-3**

Joseph has been forgotten. These are the striking words found in the opening chapters of the Book of Exodus. Along with Joseph, the God of Joseph has been forgotten as well. The new Pharoah over Egypt has no regard for God or His people. In fear, he does his best to put an end to them. But no plan of man can overcome the promise of God. He will deliver them back to the Promised Land through Moses.

Day Three: **Exodus 4-6**

A new leader of God's people has been selected. Moses is an unlikely leader, but that is God's pattern so far. Moses is a murderer and a poor public speaker. What could possibly qualify him to lead an exodus of God's people? The answer to that question is the point. Only God could call such a man and be successful. Therefore, only God can get credit for what is about to happen.

Day Four: **Exodus 7-9**

A war of gods is underway. On one corner stands the God of Abraham, Isaac, Jacob, and Moses. On the other stands the pantheon of gods that Egypt worships. Each plague that God sends on Egypt for Pharaoh's hard heart is a direct attack on the various gods that they worship. This is more than a physical encounter of nations. It is a spiritual fight of the gods, of which there can be only one victor.

Day Five: **Exodus 10-12**

The slow destruction of Egypt was not enough to shake Pharoah and open his eyes to the power of God. But there is one thing that Pharoah could not ignore: death. The final plague of God on Pharoah and Egypt's sinfulness was the death of the firstborn. Interestingly enough, this is the only plague that requires Israel's obedience as well. This is not only a judgment of God's enemy but a refining of God's people before the exodus occurs. Take note of the Passover meal that is observed because it will play a role in God's people throughout the whole Bible.

Day Six: **Exodus 13-15**

The Lord of Israel did it! He did the impossible and delivered a defenseless people from the powerful Pharaoh. He caused His people to walk on dry land in the same place where the Egyptian army drowned. Look no further for proof that the covenant of Abraham now rests on Moses as he leads the nation of Israel through the wilderness back towards the Promised Land.

Oh, how quickly God's people forget their God. This theme emerges in the Book of Exodus and lasts for the rest of the Old Testament. Within days of such a great salvation, they begin to grumble and doubt God's ability to provide for them in the wilderness. It is good news that God is gracious and kind. He meets the needs of His people who do not deserve it.

1. What responsibility lies on God's people for allowing Joseph and their God to be forgotten in Egypt?

2. Why did God provide Aaron to help Moses when God called Moses alone to the task of leadership?

3. How do some people end up with hard hearts while others are open to God?

4. Why would God require obedience among His people for the final plague?

5. How does God's parting of the Red Sea prove He is the One true God?

6. What of Moses' song should you remember today?

What causes you to forget or doubt God's promise to provide?

How God's People Should Live

SCRIPTURE READINGS

Day One: Exodus 19-21
Day Two: Exodus 22-24
Day Three: Exodus 25-27
Day Four: Exodus 28-29
Day Five: Exodus 30-32
Day Six: Exodus 33-35
Day Seven: Exodus 36-38

SUMMARIES

Day One: Exodus 19-21

Do you remember when God made the covenant with Abraham? That was the first major event that began with God's people. In these chapters, God makes a covenant with His people again through Moses. This is not a new covenant, but an explanation of the old. It tells the people how God expects them to love and follow Him as His people.

Day Two: Exodus 22-24

These long lists of laws are putting meat onto the bare bones of the covenant with Abraham. If He is going to be their God and they are going to be His people, then they must live this way. They must worship Him alone, commit to loving one another, and be willing to sacrifice for their sins. All of God's people agreed to these terms.

Day Three: **Exodus 25-27**

In these chapters, the Tabernacle is described. This is the place where God will dwell among His people. He has specific rooms and furniture pieces that are all to be used in their worship of Him and communion with Him. The interesting thing about the Tabernacle is that it was completely mobile because God's people would be traveling to the Promised Land.

Day Four: **Exodus 28-29**

The details of God's priests come to light in this section. The priests were the ones who looked after the Tabernacle, moved it when God moved, and performed the sacrifices for God's people. They have special clothes that they wear to help them do the special work they have been called to do. These men are set apart or consecrated for God's use, just as the items in the Tabernacle were.

Day Five: **Exodus 30-32**

While Moses is receiving the Law of God on the mountaintop, God's people are up tono good in the valley. It's astonishing how quickly they give up on God and make an idol of their own to worship. They had grumbled in the wilderness up to this point. But they had yet to actually forge an idol. With gold that should have been used for the Tabernacle, they made a false god.

Day Six: **Exodus 33-35**

Moses is obviously displeased with the scene he returns to. He demonstrates his displeasure by breaking the stone tablets containing God's Law. This was to show God's people what they had done by making the golden calf. The people are disciplined for their actions, and God graciously renews His covenant and law with His people. This grace will run like a river through God's disobedient people.

As more and more details are given about the Tabernacle, you get a clearer picture of what it is to be like. What started with pictures of the overall structure has now turned to details of the furniture pieces that will be there. In a wonderful provision of God, these nomadic people have all of the resources and talent necessary to put together God's vision.

1. Why is it important for God to give His people expectations?

2. What do these laws of God teach you about Him?

3. What fault does Aaron bear for making the golden calf for Israel?

4. How would you have reacted if you were Moses and saw the golden calf?

5. What is the significance of God's desire to dwell among His people?

6. What job could you have done to help in the construction of the Tabernacle?

7. Where did Israel get all of the resources necessary to build the Tabernacle?

AUTHOR

Moses

GENRE

Law

PURPOSE:

The Book of Leviticus is a book of Law. It bears its name in light of who will be administering the rules within the book. There is a tribe that emerges from God's people called the Levites. It is their duty to perform the tasks of the priest. These were the men who were given charge of the spiritual care of God's people.

Therefore, the Book of Leviticus is a book of law that was intended to be taught by the Levites and put into practice. In this book, you will find all kinds of rules and regulations regarding sacrifices, offerings, and the physical appearance of God's people.

The purpose of these rules is two-fold. The first reason is to make it clear that God's people are sinful. They cannot keep the law perfectly, thus their need for a sacrifice. The second reason is to mark God's people as holy or distinct from the world around them. They were to look and live differently from everyone else. So that everyone else can see clearly who God is and what it looks like to follow Him.

KEY VERSE

Leviticus 20:26

The Rules of Worship

SCRIPTURE READINGS

Day One: **Exodus 39-40**
Day Two: **Leviticus 1-4**
Day Three: **Leviticus 5-7**
Day Four: **Leviticus 8-10**
Day Five: **Leviticus 11-13**
Day Six: **Leviticus 14-15**
Day Seven: **Leviticus 16-18**

SUMMARIES

Day One: **Exodus 39-40**

Finally, the moment God's people had been waiting for had arrived. All of the resources were in place, and all of the people were ready. They worked tirelessly to make God's vision a reality. And then it finally happened. The Tabernacle walls were erected, and all the pieces were in place. Wonderfully, God's glory so filled the Tabernacle, that it was dangerous to even enter into it. God made it known by His word and His presence that they are His people, and He is their God.

Day Two: **Leviticus 1-4**

As you enter into the Book of Leviticus, be warned. This is one of the hardest books to be engaged with. It is largely a list of rules and regulations regarding the sacrificial system for Israel. Much of what is said will feel foreign and strange to you. Press through it, and you will find that it will be worth it. Read it in light of the sacrifice of God's Son that is to come to see what all Jesus accomplished on the cross.

Day Three: **Leviticus 5-7**

The law surrounding the sacrifices is drawing to a close in these chapters. As you will notice, there are many ways and reasons to offer a sacrifice to God. Whether with tears of sorrowful repentance or tears of overwhelming gratitude, God's people were to come and communicate those things to Him through sacrifices and offerings. This was the primary way God's people would publicly express their worship.

Day Four: **Leviticus 8-10**

If you have doubted whether or not God takes His laws seriously, look no further than these chapters. The leaders of the worship among God's people are held to an incredibly high standard because they are handling the souls of Israel. He will not stand for half-hearted leaders who do not take it as seriously as He does. The right worship of God must be a top priority among priests.

Day Five: **Leviticus 11-13**

In the coming chapters, there is a running theme of cleanliness. What is expected spiritually of God's people, is expected physically as well. God's people were to have pure hearts as they worshiped Him. This was to be exemplified in the purity of their bodies as well. If someone ever became unclean, there were ways for them to become clean as well. This reveals to us a wonderful truth of God. You can always be cleansed again.

Day Six: **Leviticus 14-15**

The cleanliness laws are furthered in these chapters. Like with the long lists of regulations around the sacrifices, these laws can seem tedious to read. Bear this in mind as you do. Imagine how exhausting it would be to keep them all. Imagine how impossible it was to do this perfectly. Let the weight of that exhaustion and imperfection prepare your heart for the only truly pure One to come, Jesus.

If there is a chapter to highlight and make note of in the Book of Leviticus, it is chapter 16. This chapter contains the rules regarding the Day of Atonement. This annual date will be an important event in the life of Israel. It is the one day a year that the High Priest can enter all the way into the presence of God. There, he could intercede on behalf of God's people in a special way.

1. How did you feel as you read all of the laws in Leviticus?

2. Which section of laws did you struggle to understand?

3. Do you think it is right for God to take His priests' purity so seriously?

4. What do you think it would have been like being the High Priest on the Day of Atonement?

5. Why do you think cleanliness is so important to God in His Law?

6. Do any of the laws feel unfair to you?

7. Who are the spiritual leaders in your life?

Numbers

AUTHOR

Moses

GENRE

Historical Narrative

PURPOSE

As you read in the Book of Exodus, God's people struggle to trust Him. In fact, they defy and deny Him in many ways. Sadly, even through the discipline that God provides, His people do not change. The Book of Numbers continues the frustrating story of rebellion. This book highlights the sinful state of God's people as well as His long-suffering love for them.

The reason it is called the Book of Numbers will become evident quickly as you read it. Within this section of Scripture, there are long recordings of numbers. The number of people connected to various tribes and families. These numbers are for their historical records. It tells us how large God's people had grown to be and where their lineage came from.

These sections can be difficult to read and even seem pointless. But take a moment to consider how these passages give us historical reliability as we read. We can take those numbers and families and place them against what we know about history from secular resources. As we contrast and compare, we will see the reliability of God's word. Those numbers, while dull to read, carry significance.

KEY VERSE

Numbers 14:11

The History of the Wilderness

SCRIPTURE READINGS

Day One: **Leviticus 19-21**
Day Two: **Leviticus 22-23**
Day Three: **Leviticus 24-25**
Day Four: **Leviticus 26-27**
Day Five: **Numbers 1-2**
Day Six: **Numbers 3-4**
Day Seven: **Numbers 5-6**

SUMMARIES

Day One: **Leviticus 19-21**

The term 'holy' is incredibly important to understand in the Book of Leviticus. It does not simply mean 'clean' or 'pure' as much of Leviticus has been about. Holy means "to be set apart for a special purpose." When God is described as holy, it is because He is completely distinct and set apart from all of creation. When God calls His people to be holy, He calls them to live distinct, set-apart lives.

Day Two: **Leviticus 22-23**

These chapters contain more clues to understanding the rest of the Bible. Various feasts and festivals are described here that will be mentioned numerous times in Scripture. As you read, you'll want to focus more on the purpose of the events over the details of when and how they are to be observed. It's their purpose that will carry the meaning as you continue your study of God's word.

Day Three: **Leviticus 24-25**

The concept of the Sabbath was originally introduced to God's people in the Ten Commandments. It was repeated to them in the 23rd chapter of the Book of Leviticus. It isn't until these chapters that you will realize just how ingrained in God's character the concept of a Sabbath rest is. He will lay out for them a Sabbath year and a year of Jubilee. God's nature is one that prioritizes rest and forgiveness for His people.

Day Four: **Leviticus 26-27**

God always makes His expectations clear for His people. Yes, His rules are rigid and hard to follow, but God's people are never left guessing what to expect. They are never unsure of where they stand before God. God makes His relationship expectations abundantly clear in these chapters, and He expresses the blessings that accompany obedience and the punishment that follows disobedience.

Day Five: **Numbers 1-2**

As God's people travel through the wilderness to find the Promised Land, God begins to bring more structure to them. In the book of Numbers, you'll see practical lists of numbers beginning in chapter one. These were to help keep a record of how many and who was among God's people. Further, a particular arrangement of God's people is laid out.

Day Six: **Numbers 3-4**

As you continue to read your way through these chapters, you'll continue to see the formation of God's people as a society. One group you'll notice that has special rules and treatment is the Levites. As discussed before, the men in this tribe were set apart for the service of God in the temple. They were reliant on the faithfulness of God and His people for their provisions.

There are some similarities that emerge from these chapters and the book of Leviticus. These laws are repeated many times in many ways in the first five books of the Bible. These books are known as the Pentateuch. In the New Testament. These books as a whole will be referred to as "The Law."

1. What did you find difficult about reading the book of Leviticus?

2. Who can you talk to to get more information about the difficult parts to understand?

3. Why do you think God had a sacrificial system for His people?

4. What is the significance of the statement, "Be holy for I am holy?"

5. How do the records of the numbers help us know more about God's people?

6. Do you think these records validate the historical accuracy of God's Word?

7. If it was up to you, would you want to be a Levite?

AUTHOR

Many Different Authors, including Moses and David.

GENRE

Poetry

PURPOSE:

The Book of Psalms is an incredible collection of songs and poetry from God's people. They span all kinds of topics and tap into every human emotion. As you read your way through it, you'll be swept up by the passionate words.

There are psalms that are doused in fear and anger. Others that overflow with joy and gratitude. If you have experienced it in your walk with Jesus, it has been penned by a saint who has gone before us. The purpose of the Book of Psalms is to help us worship God.

It shows us that we can use all of our emotions in bringing God deep, meaningful, and honest worship. Not all psalms are bright and sunny, and neither is all worship. All worship is honest with God about who we are and who He is. With each psalm, the author will always acknowledge the greatness of God, no matter the terrible nature of their plight. There is an undertone of trust in Him, no matter what.

KEY VERSE

Psalm 29:1-2

SCRIPTURE READINGS

Day One: **Numbers 7**
Day Two: **Numbers 8-10**
Day Three: **Numbers 11-13**
Day Four: **Numbers 14-15; Psalm 90**
Day Five: **Numbers 16-17**
Day Six: **Numbers 18-20**
Day Seven: **Numbers 21-22**

SUMMARIES

Day One: **Numbers 7**

If the book of Leviticus is the script, the book of Numbers is the play. You'll now get to hear those laws and read them in action as God's temple is consecrated through the sacrifices of God's people. Remember, the point of these sacrifices was to worship God for all He had done for His people.

Day Two: **Numbers 8-10**

Hopefully, you will remember the Passover meal that was instituted when God delivered His people from Egypt. They will continue to observe this meal annually. As they do, God makes it known to His people that He is with them by covering the Tabernacle in a cloud of His glory. Everything was in place for God's people to worship Him and follow Him.

Day Three: **Numbers 11-13**

Sadly, as they did after the first Passover meal, God's people complain after the second. And their complaints haven't really changed. God's people haven't really changed. Although He has been faithful to provide, they are faithless. In spite of His incredible mercy on them, they are merciless in their attitude toward Him.

Day Four: **Numbers 14-15; Psalm 90**

God has had enough of His foolish people, and He is ready to start again. But Moses intercedes on their behalf. This means that He prays for God's continued mercy on them. Take time to read the Psalm in conjunction with the book of Numbers and hear what would have been on Moses' heart as He prayed to God.

Day Five: **Numbers 16-17**

God takes the purity of His people seriously. He will not tolerate rebellion among them, nor rebellion against Him. Punishment may be delayed by His grace, but it is sure to come. In these verses, you'll read of a swift, just punishment from a holy God. Let it remind you of His power.

Day Six: **Numbers 18-20**

The first two chapters will remind you of the Levitical laws that you have already studied. Chapter 20, however, goes back to the narrative of God's people. There, you will see more similarities with God's people immediately after the exodus. Sadly, it's not just God's people who sin, but their leader, Moses.

Day Seven: **Numbers 21-22**

There are so many wonderful stories in these chapters, but I want you to pay special attention to the story of the bronze serpent. It gives us a beautiful picture of what Jesus will do on the cross in the New Testament. Jesus Himself refers back to this story as He preaches to His followers. Just like the serpent, if we will keep our eyes fixed on Jesus, we will be saved.

1. Why do you think God's people continue to make the same mistakes?

2. Why would Moses strike the rock instead of obeying God?

3. How does the bronze serpent help you understand what Jesus did on the cross?

4. Do you think the punishment for Korah's rebellion was fair?

5. Is there someone you can intercede in prayer for?

6. Why do you think God makes His presence known after the Passover is celebrated?

7. What new thing did you learn this week in your reading?

AUTHOR

Moses

GENRE

Law

PURPOSE

The exodus, which led to the wandering and grumbling, has finally come to an end. God's people now stand on the edge of the Promised Land and seek a path forward. Part of their preparation to enter the enemy-occupied land includes scouting and assigning new leaders. But the largest portion of Deuteronomy and the biggest need for God's people is a renewal of commitment to following God's law.

The Book of Deuteronomy spends most of its ink recounting the Law given to Moses in the wilderness and stresses the importance of obedience. Essentially, it is said that the choice of obedience is one of life and death. If they follow the Lord, they will be blessed and live. If they turn away or against Him, they will find curses and death.

The purpose behind it all is to prepare God's people spiritually for what they are about to face. They will have to fight to take the land that God has promised them. They will have to remain steadfast in their God while encountering many other gods. They have a large task ahead of them.

KEY VERSE

Deuteronomy 30:19-20

SCRIPTURE READINGS

Day One: **Numbers 23-25**

Day Two: **Numbers 26-27**

Day Three: **Numbers 28-30**

Day Four: **Numbers 31-32**

Day Five: **Numbers 33-34**

Day Six: **Numbers 35-36**

Day Seven: **Deuteronomy 1-2**

SUMMARIES

Day One: **Numbers 23-25**

Because the names Balak and Balaam are so similar, and because they come out of nowhere, it can be hard to follow the story in these chapters. Take special care to read and understand who is among God's people and who is not. If you get confused, notice who is worshiping Baal (a false god) in Chapter 25.

Day Two: **Numbers 26-27**

The census of the new generation is not a very fun read, but it has incredible significance. If you can remember the story, Moses and his generation were barred from entering the Promised Land. Because of their lack of faith, they would be able to see it, but not go in. The census of the new generation marks a significant transition in the life of God's people.

Day Three: **Numbers 28-30**

As they prepare to enter the Promised Land with a new leader emerging, God's people do what they often do. With a new beginning, there is a renewal of commitment to following the laws of God.

Specifically, the laws regarding offerings are remembered and followed anew. It is as if God's people are vowing once again to be faithful to Him.

Day Four: **Numbers 31-32**

The Midianites have been a problem for God's people and will continue to be. It is interesting how God handles the enemies of His people. Sometimes, He will use them to judge His own people. Other times, He will use His people to judge the enemies. In all cases, God is being merciful to one and just towards the other.

Day Five: **Numbers 33-34**

The boundary lines are beginning to be drawn. That seems like a great moment for God's people. They are beginning to settle in. However, when God sent them to the Promised Land, it was not for a portion of it. God desires for them to inhabit it all and drive everyone else out. God is not only after a pure people, but a pure land for His people.

Day Six: **Numbers 35-36**

The book of Numbers comes to a close in a fitting way for the book. It is not an exciting story or a problem solved by the Almighty God. There are more laws and records for God's people. While this book does provide a lot of stories concerning God's people, it is definitely a book designed for historical accuracy and not intrigue.

Day Seven: **Deuteronomy 1-2**

As you end this week, you begin a brand new book. It bears a new name and begins in a new chapter, but it continues the same story. As God's people settled in before taking all of the land, they became satisfied with less than what God had for them. This may give you flashbacks of the Tower of Babel. The same basic sin is being committed, and God will drive them towards obedience again.

1. Why do you think the foreign king wanted the God prophet to bless them?

2. What is the significance of a donkey being the mouthpiece for God?

3. How do you predict Joshua will do as a leader among God's people?

4. Do you think God's people will show Joshua the same respect as they did Moses?

5. Why would God's people settle before taking the whole Promised Land?

6. Why does God push them to take the whole land?

7. What themes have you noticed this week as you have read the Bible?

Love and Serve God

SCRIPTURE READINGS

Day One: **Deuteronomy 3-4**
Day Two: **Deuteronomy 5-7**
Day Three: **Deuteronomy 8-10**
Day Four: **Deuteronomy 11-13**
Day Five: **Deuteronomy 14-16**
Day Six: **Deuteronomy 17-20**
Day Seven: **Deuteronomy 21-23**

SUMMARIES

Day One: **Deuteronomy 3-4**

Repentance is one of the major themes of the Bible. This is where you turn from your evil ways and turn back to God. You have already read about many accounts of repentance, and here is another. Moses, upon losing his opportunity to enter into the Promised Land, repents and calls all of Israel to seek God first.

Day Two: **Deuteronomy 5-7**

God's people are called a holy nation for many reasons. However, the heart of it is found in these chapters. They are set apart because they follow a unique set of laws given to them by God. And they are distinct because they have been chosen among all other nations. God's choice of them was pure grace. They had not earned His love. He simply gave it.

Day Three: **Deuteronomy 8-10**

The issue that God's people faced then is the same that God's people face now. We can get caught going through the motions of worship and obedience without having the right heart and motivation. In these chapters, the Lord makes it clear that He wants heart obedience more than anything else.

Day Four: **Deuteronomy 11-13**

The Christian life can be summarized as it is in chapter 11. We are to love and serve the Lord. No matter what job we hold, how big our family is, or what position we have in our local churches, we all have the same basic tasks. If we will spend every moment of our days trying to serve and love Him, we will keep ourselves from all kinds of heartache.

Day Five: **Deuteronomy 14-16**

As you read your way through these chapters, you'll notice a lot of repetition. God's law is recorded in many different books. This is for a few reasons. The first is because it was emphasized at different times. The second is because each time adds a level of clarity to God's people. And finally, one of the most important practices of God's people was to record and memorize His law.

Day Six: **Deuteronomy 17-20**

These chapters all consider leadership and how they are to act as a nation. You'll see laws for kings be laid out. However, Israel has no king, save God Himself. These laws are preemptive of what is to come among His people. All of these laws and regulations are to help prepare them for the challenges they will face as they enter into war to take the Promised Land from its inhabitants.

Like with the book of Leviticus, there are a bunch of rules to wade your way through. Don't give up on reading Deuteronomy! Rather, press forward and consider the great grace that Christians are no longer under the law, but under the Spirit. Each of these laws was perfectly kept by Jesus. His perfection is seen in place of our failures.

1.   Why is repentance an important part of the Christian life?

2.   What is a sin that you need to repent of?

3.   In what ways can you love God more this week?

4.   How can you serve God in your local church?

5.   Why do you think God gave rules regarding kings far before they were needed?

6.   Who do you think the "new prophet" like Moses will be?

7.   Why do God's people need a new or greater prophet?

AUTHOR

Joshua

GENRE

Historical Narrative

PURPOSE

The Book of Joshua records a major transition in the life of God's people. Their faithful leader, Moses, has passed the torch to Joshua. Because of his own sin, Moses was not permitted to enter into the Promised Land. Joshua would be the one who would lead God's people on this seemingly impossible military campaign.

As you read this piece of Israel's history, you'll experience incredible stories of God's mighty hand at work. You'll hear of the sad failures of God's people to trust Him, despite His never failing faithfulness to them. You'll notice many similarities between Moses' leadership and Joshua's. Both will cross a great river; both will enter into enemy territory; both will deal with grumbling people who will not keep the Law of God.

The overall purpose of this book is to record and show how God kept His promise. Many years ago, He promised to give to the descendants of Abraham a great land. And now, God is leading them through the wartorn path to keeping that promise.

KEY VERSE

Joshua 1:6-9

Life and Death

Day One: **Deuteronomy 24-27**

Day Two: **Deuteronomy 28-29**

Day Three: **Deuteronomy 30-31**

Day Four: **Deuteronomy 32-34; Psalm 91**

Day Five: **Joshua 1-4**

Day Six: **Joshua 5-8**

Day Seven: **Joshua 9-11**

SUMMARIES

Day One: **Deuteronomy 24-27**

In these chapters, you'll learn of a giving practice that is still used in the local church. It is called tithing. Its roots are found in the Old Testament, but have been reinterpreted for the Church in the New Testament. Some may hold tightly to the ten percent figure that the original tithe is based on, but the clear teaching of the New Testament is that we are to give cheerfully and systematically to the local church.

Day Two: **Deuteronomy 28-29**

So many of the Old Testament prophets are going to make references back to these chapters. The concept of blessings for obedience and curses for disobedience never goes away. Soak in these chapters and see the justice of God. He has a great love and care for His people. So much so that He will not allow them to go without discipline.

Day Three: **Deuteronomy 30-31**

Following God, at the end of it all, is a choice between life and death. To follow Him and find His blessings will end in the ultimate blessing of everlasting life. To reject His commands and disobey ends in the ultimate curse of everlasting death. Feel the weight of these truths as you read today.

Day Four: **Deuteronomy 32-34; Psalm 91**

Chronologically speaking, Psalm 91 was probably written around the time of Deuteronomy. As Deuteronomy comes to a close, you can understand the heartbeat of the Psalm. Where else can God's people go for refuge? Who else can keep them safe as they journey into the Promised Land? It must be none other than God Himself.

Day Five: **Joshua 1-4**

A new leader has risen up among God's people. Joshua was appointed earlier in Deuteronomy, installed at the end of the book, and now begins his term as leader. It is interesting to see the similarities between the Exodus and Joshua's entrance into the Promised Land. They, too, send in spies and have to cross the river.

Day Six: **Joshua 5-8**

Blessings and cursings, life and death, both realities that were foretold, are now seen in these chapters. In one battle, God's people were faithful to His leadership. They won the war and were saved through it all. In the following battle, they were disobedient, and they paid the price for it. This ought to serve as a warning for upcoming battles for God's people.

Day Seven: **Joshua 9-11**

Nothing will keep God's armies from victory if He has ordained the battle. From the mass confusion of the enemy to stopping the sun in its tracks, God's plans will not be thwarted. Take comfort in that today, friend. Whatever God has planned for your day and whatever He calls you to, He will see you through it.

1. Do you give regularly to your local church? Why or why not?

2. What blessings for obedience stand out to you?

3. What curses for obedience stand out to you?

4. Do you consider your walk with God a matter of life and death?

5. How would you feel if you were the new leader of God's people?

6. Have you ever had to show a Jericho-like faith in life?

7. How do you predict the conquest of the Promised Land will end?

AUTHOR

Samuel

GENRE

Historical Narrative

PURPOSE:

The purpose of the Book of Judges is to shed light on the changing government of God's people. With the passing of Joshua, another leader was needed. Since God's people had ended their conquest of the Promised Land, they needed a new kind of leader. They didn't need someone to forge a new path. They needed someone to help them settle in.

These leaders were called Judges. They were there to help God's people decide between right and wrong. They made governmental decisions for God's people. But don't be fooled. Most of the judges still knew their way around a sword. This book records some incredible stories of impossible fights.

The key to understanding the Book of Judges is to take note of the cycle that happens over and over again. God's people reject Him and make their own way. God then punishes them. They cry out to Him for deliverance and forgiveness. He sends a judge and delivers them. Rinse and repeat. Each time through the cycle, their commitment to Him lessens, and His punishment of them increases.

KEY VERSE

Judges 2:16-19

The Conquest of Canaan

SCRIPTURE READINGS

Day One: **Joshua 12-15**

Day Two: **Joshua 16-18**

Day Three: **Joshua 19-21**

Day Four: **Joshua 22-24**

Day Five: **Judges 1-2**

Day Six: **Judges 3-5**

Day Seven: **Judges 6-7**

SUMMARIES

Day One: **Joshua 12-15**

God has been faithful. Tribe by tribe and city by city, God's people have been able to take the Promised Land. A list of conquered kings is recorded in these chapters. The remaining land is listed. And the conquered land is already being divided among the various tribes of Israel. Like before they entered the Promised Land, the temptation to settle for less than God's provision is entering.

Day Two: **Joshua 16-18**

The final allotments to the remaining tribes are recorded in these chapters. You may struggle to understand the geographical significance of some of them. I would encourage you to see if there are biblical maps in the back of your Bible. Most Bibles will have them. If not, take time to search the maps online to gain a better understanding.

Day Three: **Joshua 19-21**

The final people provided for in the new land allotments are those who seek refuge and the Levites. God provides in a special way for both groups. Those seeking refuge will find it among God's people.

The spiritual leaders, the Levites, will be provided for by the generosity of God's people. These people groups will not be neglected.

Day Four: **Joshua 22-24**

Like Moses, Joshua leads God's people to renew their covenant commitments to God. This should show us an important part of what it means to follow Jesus. Although we love and trust Him, there is a need in our hearts to recommit to Him. We must daily decide to follow Him and seek to do better than the day before.

Day Five: **Judges 1-2**

The Book of Judges introduces another season of life for God's people. Up until this point, they have been led through the wilderness or into battle by one main leader. Now, God's people have settled with less than God has provided. As they settle, God sends judges to spur them toward righteousness and deliver them from evil.

Day Six: **Judges 3-5**

Four different judges' stories are told in the chapters. The most notable is that of Deborah. Every leader of God's people up to this point has been a man. Deborah is the first female to hold an official title as a clear leader. She does not lead alone, as Barak is her right-hand man, but she is clearly marked as the judge.

Day Seven: **Judges 6-7**

The cycle continues over and over in Judges. God's people sin. God punishes them. God's people cry out for help. God delivers them through a judge. Even after incredible victories like Gideon sees, they still fall away. Oh, how fickle and forgetful the human heart is. But praise God that He is always faithful to deliver us from evil in the end.

1. How did looking at a map of ancient Israel help you to understand the Scripture?

2. What did you learn about God's heart about those who seek refuge?

3. Why would God make the tribe of Levi dependent on the other tribes?

4. Why would Israel stop their military action before they took the whole Promised Land?

5. What is the significance of Deborah being the first female leader of God's people?

6. How can you relate to Gideon's fear?

7. When has God proven to you His faithfulness?

AUTHOR

Samuel

GENRE

Historical Narrative

PURPOSE

As you begin reading this book, you'll wonder why it's in the Bible. On the surface, it seems to be an endearing love story, which is sweet but seems out of place. Before and after this book, you have books of war and great leadership. Why is Ruth shoved into the cracks between Judges and 1 Samuel?

All of it is made clear at the very end of the book. Ruth was not one of God's people. However, by God's providence, she was brought into God's people by marriage. She experiences deep pain as her husband dies at a young age, and she is faced with a hard choice. She can return home and try to start over, or she can stay in the people of God.

She chooses a life of godliness and becomes the great-grandmother of King David. The story of Ruth is beautiful. It shows sacrificial and redemptive love among God's people. Its place among the larger books of the Bible should not be questioned. It provides a key back story to the story of King David's family to come.

KEY VERSE

Ruth 1:16

AUTHOR

Samuel

GENRE

Historical Narrative

PURPOSE:

One more major transition takes place among the leaders of God's people. As they continue to settle into the Promised Land, they look around and see that they are the only nation without a king. They demand one from the One True King, God Himself. After receiving warning after warning, they do not relent. God gives them over to this destructive desire.

The Books of 1 and 2 Samuel are meant to be read as one big story. They are two parts to the same story: how King David came into power and how the kingdom split in the end. Three great kings' stories are followed: Saul, David, and Solomon.

There is a theme of pride and humility throughout the Books. Pride leads to the downfall of all three kings. In fact, all of the kings of Israel will struggle with this basic sinful tendency. It is the humble who receive the blessings and protection of God. There is much for us to learn about godly leadership in these books.

KEY VERSE

1 Samuel 8:6-7; 2 Samuel 7:16

The Judge Delivers

SCRIPTURE READINGS

Day One: Judges 8-9
Day Two: Judges 10-12
Day Three: Judges 13-15
Day Four: Judges 16-18
Day Five: Judges 19-21
Day Six: Ruth 1-4
Day Seven: 1 Samuel 1-3

SUMMARIES

Day One: Judges 8-9

In these stories, the teaching of Proverbs is seen plainly. God controls the hearts of kings like rivers of water. Abimelech's evil ways and scheming will not pan out for him in the end. While God allows him to dig his own grave, He does not bury him until later in the story. God typically allows evil to reign for a moment before putting it to an end.

Day Two: Judges 10-12

You've seen the cycle of God's people turn over a handful of times in the Book of Judges. However, you'll need to notice that each cycle is more dramatic. Each punishment is more painful, and each deliverance is more glorious. Each cycle is building towards its climatic end in the life of the final major judge, Samson.

Day Three: Judges 13-15

The significance of Samson's life is wrapped up in the Nazarite vow. In this vow, the individual is not supposed to partake of any wine, touch any dead thing, or cut his hair. Samson is blessed by his obedience with supernatural strength. Even when he breaks the vow regarding wine and touching dead things, God continues to provide him with strength. But there is a breaking point in the patience of God.

Day Four: **Judges 16-18**

Samson does not resist the temptation of Delilah. He allows her the knowledge of his hair, and it ends in his demise. God was so patient with Samson, but he pushed it to a breaking point. However, the grace of God did not leave Samson. You'll notice before his incredible sacrifice, his hair began growing back. This is a sign of a renewal of the vow.

Day Five: **Judges 19-21**

God's people are falling apart at the seams. The Promised Land was supposed to be a safe haven for them once they conquered it all. However, there has been nothing but strife since they did not complete the conquest. Now, their wars are not just without but within. If something doesn't change, it will dissolve. They need a greater Judge to come.

Day Six: **Ruth 1-4**

In between the great book of history rests this short story regarding a foreign woman named Ruth. The significance of this woman's life cannot be overlooked. God uses drought, famine, and death to bring Ruth into the promised land. He uses the redemption process to make her a part of His people. And ultimately, she becomes the great-grandmother of the greatest king of Israel.

Day Seven: **1 Samuel 1-3**

A new era is arising among God's people. In this new era, the leadership focus is taken off of the judges. There are no priests at the center of the story, with kings to come. The governmental structure foretold in the laws of Deuteronomy is about to come into effect. And it all begins as many things do in the Bible: a miraculous birth.

1. Which of the judges did you relate the most to?

2. How does God's control of kings make you feel?

3. Do you think you would be able to keep the Nazarite vow?

4. How many times did Samson break the Nazarite vow?

5. Why do you think that cutting his hair was the breaking point of God's grace?

6. What is the significance of his hair growing back being recorded in Scripture?

7. What does Samson's sacrificial death remind you of in the New Testament?

SCRIPTURE READINGS

Day One: **1 Samuel 4-8**
Day Two: **1 Samuel 9-12**
Day Three: **1 Samuel 13-14**
Day Four: **1 Samuel 15-17**
Day Five: **1 Samuel 18-20; Psalm 11, 59**
Day Six: **1 Samuel 21-24**
Day Seven: **Psalm 7, 27, 31, 34, 52**

SUMMARIES

Day One: **1 Samuel 4-8**

The prized possession of God's people has been taken by the enemy. If you remember its origin, you'll recall that the Ark of the Covenant is a symbol of God's presence with His people. It would stay in the center of the Tabernacle until God led His people forward. Losing such a precious item was devastating to God's people and put them in significant danger.

Day Two: **1 Samuel 9-12**

With all of the turmoil that God's people have endured, they wanted to take matters into their own hands. They demanded a king from God. He warned them of this decision. He warned them of the troubles that would come from taking a king and rejecting Him as their King. And yet they persisted. So God gave them over to their desires.

Day Three: **1 Samuel 13-14**

Saul, up to this point, has been a godly king. He has sought to do what Samuel has instructed. He has been filled with the Spirit of God and used for His purposes. All seems to be going well until Saul loses trust in the plan of God. He takes matters into his own hands and ruins things. Ultimately, because of his actions, he will lose the kingdom to a "man after God's own heart."

Day Four: 1 Samuel 15-17

Now begins a strange transition period between the two kings. Formally, God has rejected King Saul, and He has anointed King David. However, they do not switch roles immediately. Saul is unwilling to give up the throne. With David's rising success, Saul's anger and pride rise as well. Both men, for different reasons, will begin to cry, "King me!"

Day Five: 1 Samuel 18-20; Psalm 11, 59

The Psalms interspersed in these chapters today will give you a glimpse of the heart of David. He likely wrote them around this time or at least in reflection of these events. You'll hear his genuine fear of the situation. But you'll also hear his ultimate resolve to trust in God's protection in every circumstance.

Day Six: 1 Samuel 21-24

David is on the run. Saul is chasing him down in order to take his life. Saul will go to the lengths of murder to protect his throne. David has the opportunity to take Saul's life and end the chase. But he refused to do this. He so respects the throne of God and the law of God that he will not usurp either.

Day Seven: Psalm 7, 27, 31, 34, 52

One of the many talents of King David is that he was a musician and songwriter. You have already read about the various instruments he would play for his own pleasure or for King Saul. Now, you will get to read many of the songs that he crafted. As you read, take time to think of why David would have written these things.

1. What did God's people hope to gain by getting a king?

2. Which of God's warnings against getting a king stuck out to you?

3. Why do you think Saul was not willing to wait on Samuel to offer the sacrifices?

4. Why would Saul not willingly give up the throne?

5. What does it say about God's character that He chose the youngest and smallest son to be king?

6. What kind of king would you have chosen?

7. Would David have been justified in taking Saul's life?

The Music of a King

SCRIPTURE READINGS

Day One: Psalm 56, 120, 140-142
Day Two: 1 Samuel 25-27
Day Three: Psalm 17, 35, 54, 63
Day Four: 1 Samuel 28-31; Psalm 18
Day Five: Psalm 121, 123-125, 128-130
Day Six: 2 Samuel 1-4
Day Seven: Psalm 6, 8-10, 14, 16, 19, 21

SUMMARIES

Day One: **Psalm 56, 120, 140-142**

David's life before he took the throne was tumultuous. It can be hard for us to put ourselves in his shoes. How many of us have had our lives threatened by the most powerful person in the world? Even so, David fears God more than any man. Whether Saul or Goliath, David trusts the Lord to be his refuge and strength.

Day Two: **1 Samuel 25-27**

Another opportunity comes for David to take Saul's life. This time, Samuel has passed away, and there is no one to really hold David accountable for his actions. He could get away with it. He would be praised for it by the people who followed him. But David will not lay his hands on the Lord's anointed. He trusts in God's plan.

Day Three: **Psalm 17, 35, 54, 63**

The greatness of King David and the reason he was chosen by God was not an outward think. It wasn't a physical reality that gave him the grace of God. It was a spiritual reality. David had a deep yearning for

God. Like a deer that panteth for the water, David sang that his very soul longed for the Lord. This is what made him a man after God's own heart.

Day Four: **1 Samuel 28-31; Psalm 18**

The tragic death of Saul is not only predicted in these chapters but is recorded as well. Because of his sinfulness as king, he was doomed to die a humiliating death. He could not get his own servant to assist him in the process. So he fell down on his own sword, taking his own life, so that it would not be taken from him in battle.

Day Five: **Psalm 121, 123-125, 128-130**

Song after song, we hear the deepest thoughts of David's heart on paper. Take time to make note of which songs resonate the most with you. Are there certain lines that you need to commit to memory? If you're musically inclined, set one of the songs to music and see how the Lord will use it in your own life.

Day Six: **2 Samuel 1-4**

Although David had already been anointed as king, it wasn't until Saul's death that he was able to sit on the throne. David did not rejoice at Saul's demise. Rather, he lamented the falling of the Lord's anointed. After a proper and respectable grieving period, David took the throne. This began the reign of the most important king in Israel's history, save Christ Himself.

Day Seven: **Psalm 6, 8-10, 14, 16, 19, 21**

David never ceased to praise the Lord. Not just for His mighty hand of deliverance and protection, and not just for choosing him for such a holy task, but simply for who God is. He took time to praise God for His immeasurable greatness in many of his songs. David's worship of God centered on who God is and expanded to what God had done for him.

1. Why has a book of songs been saved in the Word of God?

2. What do you notice about David's faith in his songs?

3. Take time to write a song to God today.

4. Why did David lament the death of his great enemy Saul?

5. Why is the beginning of David's reign marked with murder?

6. Have you ever felt the yearning for God that David sings about?

7. Do you sing to God on a regular basis? Why or why not?

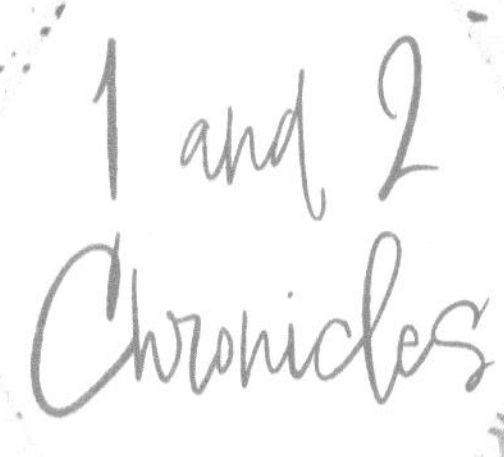

1 and 2 Chronicles

AUTHOR

Ezra

GENRE

Historical Narrative

PURPOSE

There are three sets of books that offer differing perspectives on the same period of history of God's people. These sets of books are 1 and 2 Samuel, 1 and 2 Chronicles, and 1 and 2 Kings. Each of these sets of books are to be read together as they tell the stories of the kings of God's people.

These sets all have a unique perspective to them. 1 and 2 Samuel trace the origins of the kings and highlight the united kingdom under Saul, David, and Solomon. 1 and 2 Chronicles, as well as 1 and 2 Kings, record the kings when the kingdom was split into a northern and southern kingdom.

The purpose of 1 and 2 Chronicles is to record the demise of the southern kingdom, known as Judah. Lists of kings and their successors are found with a similar refrain time after time. It is written that most of the kings did what was right in their own eyes. God would give them over to their evil desires, and they would reap the consequences.

KEY VERSE

1 Chronicles 11:1-2; 2 Chronicles 36:14

The Reign of King David

SCRIPTURE READINGS

Day One: **1 Chronicles 1-2**
Day Two: **Psalm 43-45, 49, 84-85, 87**
Day Three: **1 Chronicles 3-5**
Day Four: **Psalm 73, 77-78**
Day Five: **1 Chronicles 6**
Day Six: **Psalm 81, 88, 92-83**
Day Seven: **1 Chronicles 7-10**

SUMMARIES

Day One: **1 Chronicles 1-2**

The Book of 1 Chronicles takes a different approach to telling the story of the kings of Israel. Where 1 and 2 Samuel focused on the first three kings (Saul, David, and Solomon), 1 Chronicles zooms out and takes a look at the whole history. There is a focus on historical accuracy as the lineages are laid out for the reader.

Day Two: **Psalm 43-45, 49, 84-85, 87**

Psalm 45 is a special one in this set of psalms. Considering the war over the throne of Israel that rages between the various kings, this psalm serves as a great reminder. There is only One King among God's people. Any man who sits on the throne is subservient to God Himself. The kings of God's people would do well to keep that in mind.

Day Three: **1 Chronicles 3-5**

The records of the genealogies can be cumbersome to read. But don't forget their purpose as you read. These genealogies remind the reader of the great history of God's people. It causes us to think back to where God's people all began and how they got to where they are now. Genealogies can be a great reminder of the grace of God in the lives of His people.

Day Four: **Psalm 73, 77-78**

There are countless reasons to praise God. In just a few psalms, you will read three completely different reasons. No matter what season of life you find yourself in, God is worthy to be praised. The good days come by His hand. The bad days are kept from the worst days by His grace.

Day Five: **1 Chronicles 6**

The descendants of Levi map out the priesthood of God's people. Remember, these are the people who have no assigned land. They are dependent on the kindness of God's people for a place to live and food to eat. As you trace their names, you can trace the faithfulness and lack of faith among God's people.

Day Six: **Psalm 81, 88, 92-93**

In these psalms, you'll find the frustration of every one of God's leaders. "Oh, that my people would listen!" Moses faced grumbling in the wilderness, and David will face grumbling in his kingdom. Consider this the next time you feel like grumbling against the leadership in your church. Read these psalms the next time you're tempted in that way.

Day Seven: **1 Chronicles 7-10**

By this point, you've made it back to the point of 1 Samuel. Saul has died. David has taken over as king. As such, his story begins as the second most important king in Israel's history. Take time to appreciate the different perspective of the writing style in comparison to 1 and 2 Samuel.

1. How can the genealogies in Scripture be helpful?

2. How would we be hurt if they weren't present?

3. How do different perspectives on the same story help our understanding?

4. What is the biggest difference you noticed from 1 and 2 Samuel to 1 Chronicles?

5. Has reading the Psalms helped you gain appreciation for your church's leadership?

6. What has God taught you about Himself this week?

7. Which of the Psalms did you relate to the most this week?

A Man After God's Own Heart

SCRIPTURE READINGS

Day One: **Psalm 102-104**
Day Two: **2 Samuel 5:1-10; 1 Chronicles 11-12**
Day Three: **Psalm 133**
Day Four: **Psalm 106-107**
Day Five: **2 Samuel 5:11-25, 6:1-23; 1 Chronicles 13-16**
Day Six: **Psalm 89, 96, 100, 101, 105, 132**
Day Seven: **2 Samuel 7; 1 Chronicles 17**

SUMMARIES

Day One: **Psalm 102-104**

Psalm 103 is a great song that is worth remembering. It contains some incredible phrases of praise to God that you can use in your own personal worship of Him. Take time to read it slowly. Highlight the phrases that stand out to you as the most important. In your reading of it, bless the Lord. Let all that is in you bless His holy name.

Day Two: **2 Samuel 5:1-10; 1 Chronicles 11-12**

The anointing of David as king is recorded in many places. Each time, we should notice the significance of the moment. The original king of Israel failed. God did not pass the kingdom to Saul's son, which would have been common practice. The kingdom was given to a completely new man with a different lineage. God was changing course.

Day Three: **Psalm 133**

Unity is a highly sought-after prize among God's people. Where there is division, there comes strife. The work of God often halts when His people take their eyes off of Him and begin arguing with one another. It's no wonder that a psalm is written with unity for God's people in mind.

Day Four: **Psalm 106-107**

These psalms are being written in the midst of, or in reflection of, the events of the kings. This awareness of the context of their origin should help you to better understand and appreciate the words being used. Any time you can grasp the historical background of the books of the Bible, the more you will glean from them.

Day Five: **2 Samuel 5:11-25, 6:1-23; 1 Chronicles 13-16**

A new king has come. A new kingdom has started. And a new resting place for the Ark of the Covenant has been chosen. God is making a big point in these chapters. It is as if He is saying to Israel, "We tried it your way, and it failed. Now, watch what I can do." A new era has come under king David.

Day Six: **Psalm 89, 96, 100, 101, 105, 132**

The name of God is highly exalted in these psalms. As you meditate on them, your soul will be drawn in to join the worship of the Almighty. Many times, the steadfast love of God will be mentioned and rejoiced over. And who better to speak of His steadfast love than King David. He has surely seen it over and over again.

Day Seven: **2 Samuel 7; 1 Chronicles 17**

These chapters contain some of the most pivotal verses in all of the Old Testament. Do you remember God making a covenant with Abraham? Later, He expanded that covenant with Moses. And now, He is adding more in what's referred to as the Davidic Covenant. King David's lineage will never die, and a king from his family tree will reign forever: King Jesus.

1. What phrases in Psalm 103 stood out to you the most?

2. How does knowing the background of the kings help you understand the psalms?

3. In what ways are David and Saul similar?

4. In what ways are David and Saul different?

5. What is significant about the Ark of the Covenant being moved to Jerusalem?

6. How are the covenants God made with Abraham, Moses, and David similar?

7. How are the covenants God made with Abraham, Moses, and David different?

The Rise and Fall of David

SCRIPTURE READINGS

Day One: **Psalm 25, 29, 33, 36, 39**
Day Two: **2 Samuel 8-9; 1 Chronicles 18**
Day Three: **Psalm 50, 53, 60, 75**
Day Four: **2 Samuel 10; 1 Chronicles 19; Psalm 20**
Day Five: **Psalm 65-67, 69-70**
Day Six: **2 Samuel 11-12; 1 Chronicles 20**
Day Seven: **Psalm 32, 51, 86, 122**

SUMMARIES

Day One: **Psalm 25, 29, 33, 36, 39**

With 150 psalms preserved in the Book of Psalms and many other songs recorded in various books of the Bible, it is easy to say there are countless reasons to worship God. One thing you'll see, however, is that the reasons aren't always that different. The same reason is given on a different day. Each day, God's mercy shows up in unique ways.

Day Two: **2 Samuel 8-9; 1 Chronicles 18**

King David has started off his reign at an incredible height. Victory after victory, he experiences. This is clearly the man after God's own heart, right? Everything he touches seems to lead toward success. And as long as he will keep his heart focused on the Lord, all will be well. Sadly, not all will stay well.

Day Three: **Psalm 50, 53, 60, 75**

These psalms strike a different chord than the majority in the psalter. These strike the very fear of God in the reader. They are recognized as good and holy judges. They admit that we are not worthy to stand in His presence. This reminds us that there is a healthy fear of God for the believer. Although we are forgiven, we must remember we are not innocent.

Day Four: **2 Samuel 10; 1 Chronicles 19; Psalm 20**

David's battle with the Ammonites is laid out in these chapters. He has quite an issue with them. However, he ends the war as he always does, victoriously. As you read these stories, take note of David's leadership of his warriors and his people. There are things to be learned by this great man of God.

Day Five: **Psalm 65-67, 69-70**

God is the God of our salvation. This is a phrase that is found all throughout the Bible. But what does it really mean? It means that God is wholly responsible for our salvation. It is His standard that we have broken. It is His judgment that we are under. It is His Son who died in our place. It is His Son that is the author and perfecter of our faith. It is by His grace that we are saved.

Day Six: **2 Samuel 11-12; 1 Chronicles 20**

Lust is a killer. David's heart was swayed from the Lord and set on another man's wife. As that lust grew, death followed in its wake. No man of God, no matter how holy and righteous he may be, is immune to the sickness of sin. And once it is given an inch, it always takes a mile. Graciously, David had a godly friend to help him see the path forward.

Day Seven: **Psalm 32, 51, 86, 122**

Psalm 51 is an honest psalm that we would all do well to emulate. It asks God to search and clean out the grimy depths of our souls. As we reflect on our own condition, we quickly see how sinful we are. We might be able to fool our friends and family, but we cannot trick an all-knowing God. It would be better for us to lean on His grace than run from His discipline.

1. What is one reason you can praise God today?

2. What role do the psalms about God as judge play in our worship of Him?

3. Have you considered what it means for God to be the God of our salvation?

4. Take time to pray Psalm 51 to God. What did He show you?

5. What leadership lessons can you learn from King David?

6. Why do you think he was such a victorious king?

7. What lesson about lust can you learn from David's story?

The Hard Years for David

SCRIPTURE READINGS

Day One: **2 Samuel 13-15**
Day Two: **Psalm 3-4, 12-13, 28, 55**
Day Three: **2 Samuel 16-18**
Day Four: **Psalm 26, 40, 58, 61-62, 64**
Day Five: **2 Samuel 19-21**
Day Six: **Psalm 5, 38, 41-42**
Day Seven: **2 Samuel 22-23; Psalm 57**

SUMMARIES

Day One: **2 Samuel 13-15**

Every king will have his throne challenged from time to time during his reign. The last place you expect that challenge to come from is your own son. Your son would be the rightful heir in your passing. To have him challenge you before your death is an insult to you and to how a kingly lineage is supposed to work. And yet, this is where David finds himself in these chapters.

Day Two: **Psalm 3-4, 12-13, 28, 55**

These psalms were tear-stained in their origin. You can hear the anguish in every stroke of the pen. Desperate moments were known all too well by King David. He faced heartache in many forms. A son lost too soon, another son who tried to take his life, and everything in between. It's wonderful we have a God we can safely cry out to.

Day Three: **2 Samuel 16-18**

Can you imagine how David felt in chapter 18? If you haven't read it yet, do that first. Wow. Your son, your attempted murderer, but your son has died. How do you manage those emotions? There isn't an emotion out there that you wouldn't feel. When difficult seasons like this come, we can look to the example of King David for guidance.

Day Four: **Psalm 26, 40, 58, 61-62, 64**

"Lead me to the rock that is higher than I." What a beautiful line in an honest song from King David. Is this not what we all need from time to time? We all need a Person to be our refuge and our hiding place. The relationship that David had with God seems special and unattainable sometimes.

Day Five: **2 Samuel 19-21**

Just as David's reign began, it started again. He is a natural leader and supernaturally blessed. When God's people are on the line, David's plans are prosperous. Imagine having that kind of confidence in all of life's decisions. Imagine knowing that God is for you, no matter who or what is against you. Friend, that's true for everyone who follows Jesus.

Day Six: **Psalm 5, 38, 41-42**

Psalm 42 really captures the maturity of King David in his spiritual life. While there were many reasons for his soul to be in trouble with him, he would speak to it. He would remind his soul of the faithfulness of God. He would rest his hope in God, who had yet to let him down. Friend, that is what spiritual maturity looks like.

Day Seven: **2 Samuel 22-23; Psalm 57**

It has been said that you preach your own funeral in how you live your life. In many ways, that is true. David, in some ways, did that very thing in chapter 23. His final words were representative of his life and how God had worked in it. Like many final works, they were lasting words.

1. How would you respond if your son tried to take your throne?

2. Is there anything your child could do that would cause you not to mourn their death?

3. What can we learn from David in how he handles difficult moments in his life?

4. What psalm best captures how David felt when his son was coming after him?

5. What psalm stood out to you this week? Why?

6. What do you say spiritual maturity looks like?

7. What do you think would be said at your funeral?

SCRIPTURE READINGS

Day One: Psalm 95, 97-99
Day Two: 2 Samuel 24; 1 Chronicles 21-22; Psalm 30
Day Three: Psalm 108-110
Day Four: 1 Chronicles 23-25
Day Five: Psalm 131, 138-139, 143-145
Day Six: 1 Chronicles 26-29; Psalm 127
Day Seven: Psalm 111-118

SUMMARIES

Day One: Psalm 95, 97-99

As you read Psalm 99, you can reflect on what you've read and learned so far in the Bible. You've seen generation after generation of God's people being led by godly men. Moses and Aaron were the first of His priests. Samuel was this priest and judge hybrid. David is reigning as a great and mighty king. And the One who ties them all together is God.

Day Two: 2 Samuel 24; 1 Chronicles 21-22; Psalm 30

David's love for God cannot be denied. Even through his failures, he has been steadfast on one main thing: the will of God. In his great love for Him, he plans to build a temple. Something more permanent and more beautiful than the Tabernacle. God did not permit him to build it, but passed that responsibility to his son, Solomon.

Day Three: Psalm 108-110

Psalm 110 is a special one. The first verse of the psalm is quoted by Jesus and is understood to prove His deity. Because the Lord (God) says to my (David's) lord, the question is raised: who other than God is the Lord of the king? The answer is no one. So when Jesus quotes this Psalm and refers to Himself, He is calling Himself God, the Lord and lord of David.

Day Four: **1 Chronicles 23-25**

Part of the greatness of King David is that he was simply a great leader. With great leadership comes organization and order. You get to see some of that expressed in these chapters. These show his ability to bring order to those under his command and use them for their highest purposes.

Day Five: **Psalm 131, 138-139, 143-145**

David was deeply intune with his own soul. He was able to identify, not only that there were times of trouble in his soul but where that trouble came from. And wonderfully, he was able to point out the answer to the troubles of his soul. Each and every time, he found hope in God alone.

Day Six: **1 Chronicles 26-29; Psalm 127**

It is hard to see such a splendid season for God's people to come to an end. With the death of David, one of his sons, Solomon, is set to take the throne. The question is whether or not Solomon will follow in his father's footsteps. Will he look more like Saul than David in the end? How will the man charged with building the temple of God hold up to the pressure?

Day Seven: **Psalm 111-118**

Psalm 113 raises a wonderful question for you to ponder today, "Who is like the Lord?" Is there any other god like Him? Is there any other religion that compares to following Him? Is there another king, merciful, just and righteous? The resounding answer of the Book of Psalms and all of Scripture is, "There is no one like our God!"

1. Why is organization an important part of being a good leader?

2. What kind of pressure do you think Solomon was under as he was anointed?

3. How do you think Solomon will compare to his father?

4. Is it right to judge a person by his father's accomplishments or failures?

5. How does connecting Psalm 110 with Jesus help you understand it?

6. When your soul is troubled, who do you turn to?

7. Take time to consider the question, "Who is like our God?"

AUTHOR

Solomon

GENRE

Wisdom Poetry

PURPOSE

The Song of Solomon (or Songs, depending on your translation of the Bible) is unique from every other book in the Bible. Its theme is the love between a husband and wife. It describes everything from the chase or desire to find a wife to the physical intimacy that is experienced between the two.

It does not stop with the physical but describes the intense emotional and spiritual connection that can take place between a man and a woman. In their courtship and marriage, there are moments when their souls long for one another and are not satisfied until they have each other.

The imagery in this book can be difficult to picture because it is so foreign geographically and historically. However, if you take the time to make those mental pictures, you'll appreciate this work all the more. It will accomplish its purpose in helping you to rejoice in the great gift of marriage.

KEY VERSE

Song of Solomon 8:6-7

AUTHOR

Solomon

GENRE

Wisdom

PURPOSE

When God told Solomon He would give him whatever he wanted, Solomon asked for wisdom. He did not seek power, riches, or fame but wisdom. It's through wisdom that Solomon could follow God faithfully. It's through wisdom that Solomon could manage power, gain riches, and earn fame. Wisdom is a great gift.

Endowed with this supernatural wisdom, Solomon wrote many books of wisdom. The pinnacle of these writings is the book of Proverbs. This book is a literal book of wisdom. It contains pithy phrases and longer discourses, all containing godly wisdom for practical life. It takes knowledge and puts it into action.

The purpose of the Book of Proverbs is to help the reader to live a wise life. As Solomon says, "The fear of God is the beginning of wisdom." Solomon couches all of his practical advice in a firm theological framework. This book is a help to life and godliness.

KEY VERSE

Proverbs 1:7

The Reign of Solomon

SCRIPTURE READINGS

Day One: **1 Kings 1-2; Psalm 37, 71, 94**
Day Two: **Psalm 119:1-88**
Day Three: **1 Kings 3-4; 2 Chronicles 1; Psalm 72**
Day Four: **Psalm 119:89-176**
Day Five: **Song of Solomon 1-8**
Day Six: **Proverbs 1-3**
Day Seven: **Proverbs 4-6**

SUMMARIES

Day One: **1 Kings 1-2; Psalm 37, 71, 94**

After more warring over the throne, there is a new king in town, Solomon. He is the third king so far for God's people. The stage is set for Solomon to accomplish great things. He has a thriving kingdom to step into. He has the calling of God to build a temple for His glory. He has all the resources he needs at his fingertips.

Day Two: **Psalm 119:1-88**

This psalm is the longest in the book of Psalms by a mile. I don't mean that literally, but it can feel that way as you flip page after page only to find Psalm 119 still going. It takes the entire Hebrew alphabet and makes a corresponding verse or stanza for each letter. The incredible thing about this psalm is that it has one central focus: the word of God.

Day Three: **1 Kings 3-4; 2 Chronicles 1; Psalm 72**

With the weight of the empire hanging on his shoulders, Solomon's request for wisdom is (naturally) wise. And God clearly blesses him with wisdom as he handles an impossible situation between two women and a baby. Solomon used this supernatural wisdom in all kinds of ways during his reign.

Day Four: **Psalm 119:89-176**

This psalm concerning the importance of the word of God has powerful statements. It is said that the writer's soul is crushed with longing for the Word of God. It is said that he would have perished if it weren't for God's life-giving word. This psalm should inspire you in your journey to press on in your study of the Word of God.

Day Five: **Song of Solomon 1-8**

I hope you can take the time to appreciate this incredible work by Solomon. As someone who had many wives, his perspective on love and marriage is an interesting one. When you compare his main ideas to the overall teaching of Scripture, you'll see that the love he describes is godly to its core.

Day Six: **Proverbs 1-3**

Before rolling out a list of proverbs, Solomon begins by making his case for wisdom. He describes where it begins and where it leads. His main encouragement is that wisdom will keep us from the destruction of sin and its vices. You can read these words as a parent speaking to a child with endearing care.

Day Seven: **Proverbs 4-6**

Warnings against adultery run all the way through these chapters. Not only was this a downfall of his father, David, but it would have been a huge temptation for Solomon. You don't get as many wives and concubines as he does without being adulterous or being highly tempted toward that end. Heed the warnings of the experienced man.

1. If God were to offer you anything you asked for, what would you request?

2. Why would Solomon ask for Wisdom?

3. How does Psalm 119 change your view of God's Word?

4. Which section of Psalm 119 was significant to you?

5. What was your reaction to reading the Song of Solomon?

6. Do you think the Song of Solomon is helpful to the Christians today?

7. Why is the fear of God the beginning of wisdom?

The Wisdom of Solomon

SCRIPTURE READINGS

Day One: **Proverbs 7-9**
Day Two: **Proverbs 10-12**
Day Three: **Proverbs 13-15**
Day Four: **Proverbs 16-18**
Day Five: **Proverbs 19-21**
Day Six: **Proverbs 22-24**
Day Seven: **1 Kings 5-6; 2 Chronicles 2-3**

SUMMARIES

Day One: **Proverbs 7-9**

In these chapters, Solomon pits folly and wisdom against one another. He does this in his writings in the Book of Ecclesiastes as well. Indicative of the words themselves, wisdom is clearly the better choice. However, Solomon defends this position in a few clever ways. Don't miss the distinctions and similarities between them.

Day Two: **Proverbs 10-12**

You've entered into the final structured section of the Book of Proverbs. So far, there have been longer strings of thought and discourses that provide wisdom. After Chapter 10, it will dissolve into individual statements. These can be difficult to read because they are so isolated. Instead of a common theme of verses next to one another, look for the overall teachings.

Day Three: **Proverbs 13-15**

These isolated proverbs contain mountains of wisdom for the reader. One of the pieces of wisdom that is repeated often in my own house is, "A soft answer turns away wrath, but a harsh word stirs up anger." You'll be greatly benefitted if you'll take a few of these proverbs each week and commit them to memory.

Day Four: **Proverbs 16-18**

One of the common themes among the proverbs concerns integrity. The essential teaching is that integrity is more important than any kind of success. Any money that is gained dishonesty and any power that is wielded in a cruel way may look like the actions of a wise man. But the heart of those actions is folly and will come to light in their time.

Day Five: **Proverbs 19-21**

A pivotal verse to understand how God relates to the kings, both of Israel and not of Israel, is found in these chapters. Proverbs 21:1 says in the ESV, "The king's heart is a stream of water in the hand of the Lord; he turns it wherever he will." All of the kings are ultimately under God's hand. He will use them as He pleases.

Day Six: **Proverbs 22-24**

Another of the common themes found in Proverbs is how to view money. You'll find some wisdom concerning finances in these verses. Each one will not drive you to desire to gain more money, but to put money in its proper place. Sayings like "The rich and the poor meet together, the Lord is the Maker of them all" bring clarity to our view of riches.

Day Seven: **1 Kings 5-6; 2 Chronicles 2-3**

Take a break from the wisdom of Solomon and jump back with me to the work of Solomon. In these chapters, the preparations and the beginning of the Temple's construction are recorded. All that Solomon needed to create this immaculate building, both resources and workers, was available to him.

1. What would you say are the dangers of adultery?

2. Do you agree with how Solomon described folly?

3. Which of the proverbs have you tried to commit to memory?

4. Were there any proverbs that you disagreed with?

5. Which proverb concerning money was the most helpful to you?

6. How would you handle leading a construction project as large as the Temple?

7. Who in your life could you call on to get help on a big project God has called you to?

Solomon's Accomplishments

SCRIPTURE READINGS

Day One: **1 Kings 7; 2 Chronicles 4**
Day Two: **1 Kings 8; 2 Chronicles 5**
Day Three: **2 Chronicles 6-7; Psalm 136**
Day Four: **Psalm 134, 146-150**
Day Five: **1 Kings 9; 2 Chronicles 8**
Day Six: **Proverbs 25-26**
Day Seven: **Proverbs 27-29**

SUMMARIES

Day One: **1 Kings 7; 2 Chronicles 4**

Like the Temple, the palace of Solomon was an incredible wonder to the eyes. He spared no expense in creating a home for himself and his extensive family. After these verses, the tone will quickly shift back to the seriousness of the bigger task at hand: building the Temple. Every detail is laid out, down to the pieces of furniture.

Day Two: **1 Kings 8; 2 Chronicles 5**

These chapters record the incredible construction of the Temple of God. Upon its completion, the Ark of the Covenant and the glory of God fill its walls. It is one of the greatest moments in Israel's history. Can you imagine such a wonderful moment? The glory of the Lord was a sure sign to His people that He was present among them.

Day Three: **2 Chronicles 6-7; Psalm 136**

Solomon's dedication to the Temple marks the building as a place of worship. Prayer, repentance, and sacrifices would be regularly seen within the walls around its courtyards. It was to be a holy place for

God's people to commune with Him. Throughout Israel's history, there is no more important place in their minds than the Temple that Solomon built.

Day Four: **Psalm 134, 146-150**

You will read a fitting end to the Book of Psalms this week. Psalm 150 is short, sweet, and to the point. It puts the whole collection of worship songs into their proper perspective. The writer of that psalm calls all of creation to join in the worship of God. The wonderful words are found in it that say, "Let everything that has breath praise the Lord!"

Day Five: **1 Kings 9; 2 Chronicles 8**

Solomon's accomplishments in 2 Chronicles 8 provide an impressive list. As you consider all that he was able to do, don't miss the hand of God working behind it all. Just as Solomon's wisdom expresses in the Book of Proverbs, a king accomplishes nothing without the blessing of God Himself.

Day Six: **Proverbs 25-26**

Welcome back to the wisdom literature of Solomon. Along with his very many accomplishments, he penned the majority of this book. In these chapters, you'll find a continued collection of individual proverbs. As you read through them, consider all that Solomon faced during his reign.

Day Seven: **Proverbs 27-29**

Solomon's proverbs end in these chapters. Like the final words of anyone, pay careful attention to how he ends his collection of wise sayings. The righteousness that is achieved through wisdom comes screaming off of the pages. If the fear of the Lord is the beginning, wisdom is the medium, and righteousness is the end.

1. How do you feel about Solomon's elaborate use of resources for himself?

2. What does it say about God that His people could not be within His glory?

3. Describe what you think that moment would have looked like.

4. Of all that Solomon accomplished, what would you say was his highest achievement?

5. Which of the proverbs was most impactful for you in these final chapters?

6. Why is righteousness the end of wisdom?

7. Do you feel more prepared for righteous living after reading these proverbs?

AUTHOR

Solomon

GENRE

Wisdom Literature

PURPOSE

The Book of Ecclesiastes, in many ways, does not feel like a book of the Bible. It is written from an agnostic point of view. Solomon presents real questions that the world has about life, death, and everything in between. In the center of it all is the question for the very meaning of life.

"Vanity of vanities. All is vanity." Is the constant refrain of Solomon as he seeks answers through all kinds of avenues. But the most interesting thing about this book is not the negative and sometimes depressed view of life that it proposes. It is how it ends. After seeking meaning in every possible path, Solomon lands firmly on one central truth.

The purpose of the Book of Ecclesiastes is to think seriously about the purpose of life and arrive at the same answer as Solomon. He says that the ultimate purpose of life is to fear God and follow Him for all the days that you have. He sees the hand of God in all seasons of life and encourages us to take God's presence and power seriously.

KEY VERSE

Ecclesiastes 12:13-14

The Great Division

SCRIPTURE READINGS

Day One: **Ecclesiastes 1-6**
Day Two: **Ecclesiastes 7-12**
Day Three: **1 Kings 10-11; 2 Chronicles 9**
Day Four: **Proverbs 30-31**
Day Five: **1 Kings 12-14**
Day Six: **2 Chronicles 10-12**
Day Seven: **1 Kings 15:1-24; 2 Chronicles 13-16**

SUMMARIES

Day One: **Ecclesiastes 1-6**

Everyone struggles with finding their purpose or meaning in life. Most of us will try various avenues to find that meaning. Solomon, as king of Israel, had every possible path at his fingertips. From pleasure, to power, to passion, Solomon tried all of these things to find purpose and found them all to be lacking.

Day Two: **Ecclesiastes 7-12**

The reality of death begins to settle in for Solomon as he continues to write this book. It's the presence of an impending death that sobers him at the end of every passionate path. He ultimately decides that life under the Sun is vain unless there is Someone over the sun, God. Without Him, then all actually is vanity.

Day Three: **1 Kings 10-11; 2 Chronicles 9**

The final chapters of Solomon's life are filled with his interaction with the Queen of Sheba. How he handles himself shows both his godliness and his worldliness. Like most kings of Israel to come, there are good and bad moments in their lives. Sadly, after Solomon dies, the kingdom will literally fall apart.

Day Four: **Proverbs 30-31**

The final two chapters of proverbs contain some of the most well-known verses in the Bible. The title of a "Proverbs 31 woman" finds its roots in these chapters. The interesting part of this great book of wisdom is that it wasn't entirely written by Solomon. These last couple of chapters are proverbs written by other wise kings.

Day Five: **1 Kings 12-14**

How many kings does it take to tear a kingdom apart? The answer apparently is 4. After Solomon's death, his son takes the throne. Not long after this transition, there is a massive rift among God's people. They take sides quickly, and there is a line drawn right down the middle. The majority of God's people left the northern kingdom of Israel, leaving the southern kingdom of Judah with a new king.

Day Six: **2 Chronicles 10-12**

Not only is there civil unrest under the leadership of Rehoboam, but there is danger from outside forces. The former enemies of God's people, Egypt, have come back to seek revenge. When Israel left Egypt in the Exodus, they plundered them. Now, Egypt is returning the favor and taking all that they can.

Day Seven: **1 Kings 15:1-24; 2 Chronicles 13-16**

After the great division of God's people, the success of kings comes like rapid fire. As you read them, it will feel like all of their reigns were short-lived. And some of them were laughably short. However, don't overlook the length of the reigns that are there. Some will be substantial in length, but very little will be recorded about them.

1. What things have you tried to find meaning in life?

2. Do you agree that fearing and following God is the ultimate purpose of mankind?

3. What proverbs of the other kings were the most impactful to you?

4. Have you ever met a Proverbs 31 Woman?

5. Why did the kingdom of God's people split?

6. What could you have done to prevent the split?

7. Do you think these two kingdoms will ever reconcile?

Obadiah

AUTHOR

Obadiah

GENRE

Prophecy

PURPOSE

The Book of Obadiah is the shortest in the Old Testament. It contains only 21 verses. It is a prophecy of condemnation and judgment on the nation of Edom. Edom is a nation that is an enemy of God's people, Israel. As Israel has struggled, Edom has been there to mock and ridicule along the way.

The prophecy of God through Obadiah is one of promised judgment to come. A common phrase in the Old Testament is, "the day of the Lord." This wondrous day will be a great day of judgment when all people will stand before the Almighty God. For His enemies, this day will be a day of incredible terror. For His people, it will be their greatest hope and joy. For on that day, He will make all things right again.

The purpose of the Book of Obadiah is to give God's people hope in difficult circumstances. When our "enemies" seem to overwhelm and surround us, we can be confident that God is for us. He will protect us and fight on our behalf. And in the end, He will be our conquering King.

KEY VERSE

Obadiah 1:15

SCRIPTURE READINGS

Day One: **1 Kings 15:25-34; 1 Kings 16:1-34; 2 Chronicles 17**
Day Two: **1 Kings 17-19**
Day Three: **1 Kings 20-21**
Day Four: **1 Kings 22; 2 Chronicles 18**
Day Five: **2 Chronicles 19-23**
Day Six: **Obadiah; Psalm 82-83**
Day Seven: **2 Kings 1-4**

SUMMARIES

Day One: **1 Kings 15:25-34; 1 Kings 16:1-34; 2 Chronicles 17**

The tragic theme of the kings of God's people is that they did what was right in their own eyes. Nearly every time, this is what was an abomination in the eyes of God. Whether the king rejected God or treated Him like one of many options, they rejected the teaching of God and led His people astray.

Day Two: **1 Kings 17-19**

The height of the depravity of God's people at this point is found under the reign of Ahab. He was king, but Jezebel, his wife, was really calling the shots. Whether he or she, neither one had anything to do with God. So God sent a judge-like prophet named Elijah to set the record straight. There is only one true God of Israel.

Day Three: **1 Kings 20-21**

Even after God's incredible display of power, King Ahab did not turn from his wicked ways. As with any king, this would be his ultimate demise. While it may have gone well for him for a short season,

God's judgment stands. Anyone leading His people will not be allowed to do whatever they please without repercussions.

Day Four: **1 Kings 22; 2 Chronicles 18**

The end of one of the most wicked kings in the history of God's people comes to a close in these chapters. It can be hard to imagine God allowing this kind of leader to even come into power. We must remember that God is patient and wise beyond our understanding. It could be His grace or His judgment that kept Ahab in power.

Day Five: **2 Chronicles 19-23**

To follow the sins of King Ahab, Jehosaphat takes the throne. Unlike his predecessor, Jehosaphat brings about some much-needed reforms in God's kingdom. Those reforms did not fix everything, and they did not last forever, but they at least put God's people back on the right track for a little while.

Day Six: **Obadiah; Psalm 82-83**

Even on their worst day, God will not turn His back on His people. Remember how it all began. God chose, grew, protected, and plated His people in the Promised Land. When they rejected Him, He kept them as the apple of His eye. While they endured punishment and judgment, God would not allow them to stay beaten forever.

Day Seven: **2 Kings 1-4**

The great prophet Elijah's ministry is coming to an end, and his successor asks for a double portion of his spirit. God grants him this kindness, and it is proven in his ministry. He reproduced many of the miracles that Elijah did during his lifetime and to a greater degree. Elisha is the new spokesperson for God.

1. Why do you think the throne of Israel kept getting more sinful?

2. What does it say about Ahab's character that Jezebel had such influence?

3. What kind of fears do you think Elijah felt in his interactions with Ahab?

4. Why do you think the reforms of Jehosaphat did not last?

5. What reforms would you have made?

6. How would you lead God's people to turn away from other gods?

7. Do you think Elisha will carry the title of prophet well?

AUTHOR

Jonah

GENRE

History/Prophecy

PURPOSE

Jonah is unlike the other prophetic books. Where prophets like Obadiah, Isaiah, and Ezekiel all focus on the message of the prophet, Jonah's writings center around the person of the prophet. Jonah's interactions with God and his calling are the central point of the book and not the call to repentance for Nineveh.

In Jonah's fear, he fled from the mission of God. In all of his running away, he found his life and the lives of those around him in great danger. Only from the lowest point in his life did he cry out to God in repentance. God saved him and gave him the same original calling.

The purpose of Jonah is to teach us two main things about God. The first is that He is incredibly patient and gracious with us. He withholds punishment often for our sake. The second is that no one, not even His prophet, will thwart His plans. He would not let Jonah go from his mission to prophesy to Nineveh.

KEY VERSE

Jonah 3:10

Isaiah

AUTHOR

Isaiah

GENRE

Prophecy

PURPOSE

The Book of Isaiah is one of the longest books in the Bible. It reveals to the reader God's judgment and His salvation. His prophetic book can be broken into two sections. While the first half reeks of judgment, the second half has the sweet aroma of salvation.

At the crux of it all, you'll find one of the most precious chapters in all of Scripture. It is the place where judgment and salvation meet, the song of the Suffering Servant. As you read Chapter 53, let your mind run to the cross of Jesus Christ. In that chapter, many prophecies are made of what Jesus will ultimately endure.

This chapter predicts the very Gospel message. God will place the judgment that God's people have earned on His own Son, the Suffering Servant. By His death, God's people will be saved. The difficulties of reading and processing this great book is all worth it when you find this wonderful chapter.

KEY VERSE

Isaiah 65:25

SCRIPTURE READINGS

Day One: **2 Kings 5-8**
Day Two: **2 Kings 9-11**
Day Three: **2 Kings 12-13; 2 Chronicles 24**
Day Four: **2 Kings 14; 2 Chronicles 25**
Day Five: **Jonah 1-4**
Day Six: **2 Kings 15; 2 Chronicles 26**
Day Seven: **Isaiah 1-4**

SUMMARIES

Day One: **2 Kings 5-8**

Elisha's ministry as a prophet is an incredible story to read. Note the similarities and differences between his ministry and Elijah's. He, too, had to deal with differing kings, but nothing like Elijah had to deal with. After Elijah's ministry is highlighted, we're back in the revolving throne of kings.

Day Two: **2 Kings 9-11**

King Jehu plays an interesting role in Israel's history. His reform was a violent one. He led the slaughter of Jezebel and Ahab's descendants. He destroyed the prophets and Baal. In his own way, he tries to lead God's people back to the right path. He had his own shortcomings, but this dedication to God's word was refreshing for the true believers.

Day Three: **2 Kings 12-13; 2 Chronicles 24**

The Temple had been wrecked through wars and foreign invasions. It was the shining glory of God's people, but now it stood tarnished by all that had happened. Under the leadership of the new king, Jehoash, the Temple was repaired. It was somewhat restored to its former glory. But unlike its construction, the glory of the Lord is not as prevalent.

Day Four: **2 Kings 14; 2 Chronicles 25**

Entering these chapters can feel like watching a tennis match. The author is going to go back and forth from the northern kingdom, Israel, to the southern kingdom, Judah. Each kingdom is rapidly changing kings, and it can be hard to follow. Sadly, the similarities between their ungodly behavior is all too simple to keep track of.

Day Five: **Jonah 1-4**

The prophet Jonah is someone anyone can relate to. We've all been given jobs we don't want to do. Many of us have resisted the Holy Spirit's prompting and felt the pain of running away. And many more of us have experienced the restoring grace of God. Be careful not to judge this prophet too quickly in his sin.

Day Six: **2 Kings 15; 2 Chronicles 26**

2 Chronicles 26 records Uzziah's reign in Judah. His issue summarizes every failure of every king of either Israel or Judah. Pride is the downfall of any leader. The moment we begin to think we are the most important or that we know more than God, our days are numbered. Take heed of the lessons learned from Uzziah's life.

Day Seven: **Isaiah 1-4**

The prophet Isaiah's ministry was focused on the nation of Judah. Just like most prophetic books, the sins of God's people are made clear in the first few chapters. It can feel like sitting in a courtroom and hearing the prosecutor list off the offenses of the accused.

1. What is the significance of the restoration of the Temple?

2. What does it mean when the glory of God is no longer as prevalent there?

3. Are there ways you can better track the different kings in the two kingdoms?

4. In what ways do you relate to Jonah?

5. Have you ever run away from a job God had called you to?

6. How did God bring you back to Himself?

7. What is the most scandalous sin that Isaiah says of Judah?

Amos

Amos' prophetic ministry is focused on the northern kingdom of Israel. While Israel is in a powerful position, they are spiritually compromised. All the money, power, and prestige cannot keep them safe from the discipline of God.

God's judgment is said to be pointed at all of God's people and the surrounding nations. In a Noahic-like moment, all the earth seemed to be filled with wickedness. And just like the ark saved a remnant of righteous men, God would ultimately restore His people.

The Book of Amos promises a happy ending. After the judgment, God would bring His people back. He would not leave them in their destruction but would bring them back. The kings that had led them astray would be replaced by a greater King to come. He would be a Messiah that would reign over the world forever.

AUTHOR

Micah

GENRE

Prophecy

PURPOSE

Micah's sights are set on the leadership of Israel. They were treating their people like wolves treat sheep. Taking advantage of the poor and helpless, misleading the people, and twisting the laws to serve themselves were the hallmarks of the leadership.

You have seen that God will not stand for kings to treat His people that way. Neither will he tolerate princes and governors to abuse their authority. This prophecy of Micah puts the leaders in the hot seat and promises them consequences for their poor work.

However, since God is gracious and kind, He does not leave His people without hope. The Book of Micah contains prophecies of a coming Shepherd who would not take advantage of the sheep. He would be a great leader who is steadfast and merciful. And He would follow God, who pardons sins and forgives. His name is Jesus.

KEY VERSE

Micah 6:8

SCRIPTURE READINGS

Day One: **Isaiah 5-8**

Day Two: **Amos 1-5**

Day Three: **Amos 6-9**

Day Four: **2 Chronicles 27; Isaiah 9-12**

Day Five: **Micah 1-7**

Day Six: **2 Chronicles 28; 2 Kings 16-17**

Day Seven: **Isaiah 13-17**

SUMMARIES

Day One: **Isaiah 5-8**

The imagery of God's people presented here is one of a vineyard. This is a common analogy that is used throughout the Bible. Jesus Himself will say that He is the vine, and we are the branches. It would be worth your time to do some research about vineyards and how they work.

Day Two: **Amos 1-5**

God takes all sin seriously. He will obviously punish the sins of the enemies of His people. But He will not withhold punishment from His own people. In His holiness, he cannot and will not tolerate rebellion of any kind. This leaves us with only one option: "Seek the Lord and live" because "justice will roll down."

Day Three: **Amos 6-9**

While a holy God will not overlook sin, He is a merciful God too. With each prophecy of judgment, a promise of restoration always follows. It is a wonderful truth that even hundreds of years after God promises to be the God of Abraham's people, He never relents. This is true, especially when His people have not earned His kindness.

Day Four: 2 Chronicles 27; Isaiah 9-12

Isaiah contains a classic Christmas passage of Scripture that says, "For to us a child is born, to us a son is given; and the government shall be upon his shoulder, and his name shall be called Wonderful Counselor, Mighty God, Everlasting Father, Prince of Peace." We hear this and think of Jesus in a manger. But when it was written, they were thinking of a mighty king!

Day Five: Micah 1-7

The Book of Micah brings to light an important thing for any Christian to consider: leadership matters. The leaders of God's people in Micah's day were corrupt and abusive towards their people. God would not stand that kind of treatment then, and He will not tolerate it now. Leadership in our churches matters.

Day Six: 2 Chronicles 28; 2 Kings 16-17

Idolatry is a never-ending problem for God's people. As early as their wandering through the wilderness to modern-day church services, idolatry is an evil snare. It is when something or someone is regarded as more important as God. These idols can be good things that become God's things.

Day Seven: Isaiah 13-17

As we have seen, God will use foreign nations to judge His own. However, He will not pass them as guiltless. In these chapters, you will read various oracles about the surrounding cities and nations. Notice the similarities between the indictments against God's people and God's enemies.

1. How does the imagery of the vineyard help you understand Isaiah?

2. God's serious tone towards sin reveals what about His character?

3. How does the Isaiah 9 Christmas passage sound different when reading it in context?

4. Why does God hold the leadership of His people to such high standards?

5. What kind of leaders do you have in your local church?

6. What idols exist in your life?

7. How can you remove the idols in your life?

AUTHOR

Hosea

GENRE

Prophecy

PURPOSE

The prophecy of Hosea is unique in how God expresses His message to His people. Typically, he just sends a prophet into the cities and Temple to proclaim His coming judgment or mercy. It is often a loud cry in the street for repentance before it's too late. This time, however, the Lord takes a different approach.

God tells Hosea to marry a woman named Gomer. She is a promiscuous woman who is prone to being unfaithful. God tells Hosea to marry her and remain married to her, no matter how adulterous she becomes. This picture of a faithful husband's commitment to his unfaithful wife is used to show how God feels about Israel.

The purpose of the Book of Hosea is to show God's people that their sins against Him are like breaking a marriage covenant. Each sinful thought and action is deeply personal to Him because He is fully committed to them. Even in the depths of their sinfulness, God always provides an avenue of restoration.

KEY VERSE

Hosea 6:6

Isaiah's Ministry in Judah

SCRIPTURE READINGS

Day One: **Isaiah 18-22**

Day Two: **Isaiah 23-27**

Day Three: **2 Kings 18:1-8; 2 Chronicles 29-31; Psalm 48**

Day Four: **Hosea 1-7**

Day Five: **Hosea 8-14**

Day Six: **Isaiah 28-30**

Day Seven: **Isaiah 31-34**

SUMMARIES

Day One: **Isaiah 18-22**

Before God's people can become too comfortable with the judgments against their enemies, God reminds them of their own coming punishment. Yes, they will be blessed in the end. But they will endure the discipline that they have earned. Indeed, all of the earth will be judged in the mighty Day of the Lord.

Day Two: **Isaiah 23-27**

The sweetness of the Gospel message rings clearly in these chapters. After the promise of coming judgment for the whole earth comes the promise that, for God's people, death will be swallowed up forever. Those who wait on the Lord will have perfect peace and redemption in the end.

Day Three: **2 Kings 18:1-8; 2 Chronicles 29-31; Psalm 48**

During the prophetic ministry of Isaiah, Hezekiah is the king of Judah. The nation that Isaiah is preaching judgment toward is being led by this king. Bear that in mind as you read their interactions with one another in these chapters. See how the context of the 2 Kings and Chronicles helps you understand the Book of Isaiah.

Day Four: **Hosea 1-7**

God's people have been spiritually promiscuous. They have given themselves over to other gods while trying to keep a relationship with the One True God. That's like having many boyfriends or girlfriends while also trying to keep a healthy relationship with your spouse. It simply won't work and didn't work for Israel.

Day Five: **Hosea 8-14**

The mixture of deep love and impending punishment runs throughout the book. The punishment, at this point, is inescapable. No amount of repentance or returning will stop the Assyrian army from crashing down on them. But in His great love, God promises also to restore His people after the judgment.

Day Six: **Isaiah 28-30**

Many times, God's people have sought refuge among foreign nations. And many times, those foreign nations have turned out to be their enemies. God cries out to His people to heed His warning and remember their past. Running into the hands of the enemy will only end in disaster.

Day Seven: **Isaiah 31-34**

All throughout the prophecy of Isaiah, there are foretellings of a great leader, king, and deliverer. There is someone who will make all things right. In these chapters, he is described as a king who will reign in righteousness. This king's name will be Jesus, the rightful ruler of all creation.

1. What have you learned about God's character from reading Isaiah?

2. What hope have you found in Isaiah's prophecies?

3. How did reading the historical context in 2 Kings and 2 Chronicles help you understand Isaiah?

4. What information did you wish you had to understand more?

5. Why do you think so many references are found in Isaiah to Jesus?

6. Do you think these prophecies of Jesus would have been obvious to the readers on that day?

7. Why do you think Israel is tempted to seek refuge in foreign nations?

The Folly of Idols

SCRIPTURE READINGS

Day One: Isaiah 35-36
Day Two: Isaiah 37-39; Psalm 76
Day Three: Isaiah 40-43
Day Four: Isaiah 44-48
Day Five: 2 Kings 18:9-37; 2 Kings 19:1-37; Psalm 46, 80, 135
Day Six: Isaiah 49-53
Day Seven: Isaiah 54-58

SUMMARIES

Day One: Isaiah 35-36

The stories of 2 Kings and 2 Chronicles are fully present in these chapters. As you go back and forth between these three books, you'll be able to get the full picture of what is going on. Having many perspectives on the same event can be incredibly helpful in your understanding of it.

Day Two: Isaiah 37-39; Psalm 76

Hezekiah's reign during the ministry of Isaiah takes up more chapters than that of any other single king. This ought to make you stop and consider the reason for it all. Think of why this king's reign would be so important to the overall message of judgment and salvation to God's people in Isaiah.

Day Three: Isaiah 40-43

Yet another reference is found to Jesus in these chapters. Chapter 42 is one of a handful of "servant songs." Scholars have given these sections of Isaiah this title because each one describes a coming Servant who will deliver God's people. Each song examines a different aspect of what that salvation will look like.

Isaiah 44-48

I love the chapters here on idolatry. They make this common sin laughable. Take time to note the inherent humor in how God addresses this problem through the prophet Isaiah. Then, take time to consider what kind of modern-day idols you have for yourself. They are just as foolish as the ones of Israel's day.

Day Five: 2 Kings 18:9-37; 2 Kings 19:1-37; Psalm 46, 80, 135

These chapters zoom back out to see where the prophecy of Isaiah is taking place. This can help remind us that these were real-life situations with real-life people involved. Sometimes, when reading the prophetic books, you can become detached from the persons who are involved in it all.

Day Six: Isaiah 49-53

You've finally made it! The greatest chapter in all of Isaiah. And arguably, the greatest chapter in the entire Old Testament is Chapter 53. This is a servant song often called "The Suffering Servant." The name will make itself obvious as you read the sacrificial work of the Servant to come to Jesus.

Day Seven: Isaiah 54-58

Fittingly so, the suffering servant makes way for the eternal covenant of peace, the great compassion of the Lord. God's grace is so abundant in these chapters it will be impossible for the believer to read them and not worship His great and holy name.

1. How have the servant songs helped you better understand who Jesus is?

2. What part of chapter 53 stood out to you?

3. Can you see how chapter 53 describes the crucifixion of Jesus?

4. What modern-day idols did you think of when reading Isaiah?

5. Why are idols so foolish in God's eyes?

6. As you step back and read the gracious plan of God to save His people, how will you worship Him today?

7. Which chapter of Isaiah has been the hardest for you to relate to?

Nahum

Nahum

Prophecy

Do you remember the prophet Jonah? After all of his running, he ended up preaching a message of repentance to Nineveh. And they listened to him! Many of them repented that day, and the Lord was pleased with it all.

Jump ahead 150 years, and you'll see that Nineveh has done what we all do. They went back to their old ways of idolatry. And so the Lord has sent another prophet to call them back to repentance. This man's name is Nahum. He is the self-proclaimed comforter of Israel during his prophetic ministry.

The message that you never really got to hear from the Book of Jonah, you hear loud and clear under Nahum. The same problems call for the same remedies. God's word spoken through God's servant hitting the hearts of God's people is how it all works.

KEY VERSE

Nahum 1:7

AUTHOR

Zephaniah

GENRE

Prophecy

PURPOSE

The Day of the Lord is a common term in the Old Testament. It refers to the day when the world's normal activities will cease. On that day, the Lord will bring judgment on all the earth. It will be a terrible and terrifying day for all mankind.

This ominous Day of the Lord is described in great detail in the prophetic ministry of Zephaniah. There is an urgency in his message as he heralds this awe-inspiring message. Since the Day of the Lord is coming, there was only one hope for God's people. That hope was God Himself.

The purpose of the Book of Zephaniah is to strike a holy fear in the hearts of God's people so that they will trust in only Him in the end. No matter how prosperous they become as a nation, only God can save them from God. Therefore, they must "seek the Lord and do what he commands."

KEY VERSE

Zephaniah 2:3

Major and Minor Prophets

SCRIPTURE READINGS

Day One: **Isaiah 59-63**
Day Two: **Isaiah 64-66**
Day Three: **2 Kings 20-21**
Day Four: **2 Chronicles 32-33**
Day Five: **Nahum 1-3**
Day Six: **2 Kings 22-23; 2 Chronicles 34-35**
Day Seven: **Zephaniah 1-3**

SUMMARIES

Day One: **Isaiah 59-63**

The final chapters of Isaiah look ahead to the future of Israel. There are incredible promises to behold and terrible judgment to fear. The coming Day of the Lord is balanced out by the year of the Lord's favor. Take your time and take it all as you read these great chapters.

Day Two: **Isaiah 64-66**

Today, you will finish the longest prophetic book in the Old Testament. There are incredible things to behold and hard sayings to work through. Through and through, the book has a simple message at the end. The only salvation from the coming judgment is found in a coming servant we know as Jesus.

Day Three: **2 Kings 20-21**

The interactions between Isaiah and Hezekiah have come to an end. The king is no longer on his throne, and the prophet has entered into his eternal rest. All the good work that happened under Hezekiah will pass away quickly under the wicked successors.

Day Four: 2 Chronicles 32-33

As you read these chapters and think back on yesterday's readings, you'll see a lot of similarities. However, you'll notice a different tone and perspective in the writing. Glean what you can from those differences and let them inform you of the whole story.

Day Five: Nahum 1-3

There are Major and Minor prophets in the Old Testament. The distinction between them is not a reflection of the importance of their message. Rather, the distinction highlights the length of their message. Nahum, as you can tell, is considered a Minor prophet compared to the Major, Isaiah.

Day Six: 2 Kings 22-23; 2 Chronicles 34-35

Josiah is the last good king in God's people. He leads the greatest reformation in the entire lineage of kings. His efforts restore the temple, restore right worship, restore the observance of the Passover, and various feasts. He really gets God's people back on the right track. The whole reformation centers on the recovered Word of God.

Day Seven: Zephaniah 1-3

Zephaniah's description of the Day of the Lord is terrifying. As you read the words, try to picture all of the events that he describes. Let the weight of the coming judgment burden you before you run to the Gospel. This will produce in you a healthy and holy fear of God that we are called to have.

1. What about the future, according to Isaiah, gives you hope?

2. What new information did you learn about the future?

3. Why is it important that God's word spurred the reformation of Josiah?

4. How had God's people gotten so far from His commands?

5. What significance was there in returning to the observance of the Passover?

6. How did it feel to read about the Day of the Lord?

7. What can you do to prepare for the Day of the Lord?

AUTHOR

Jeremiah

GENRE

Prophecy

PURPOSE

The Book of Jeremiah is called one written by the "weeping prophet." The sorrow of Jeremiah, as he prophecies against Judah, is palpable as you read each page. Because of their unrepentant sin and idolatry, Jeremiah is tasked with calling them to repentance. If they will turn back from their evil ways, there will be forgiveness and redemption.

However, Jeremiah recognizes in the midst of his prophecies that Judah will not repent. The judgment that is to come is a sure outcome, and so he laments all the more. This prophecy comes in full swing after the kid king, Josiah, who brought great reforms to God's people. But just as you read in the historical books, the kings following Josiah did not keep his reforms.

The purpose of the Book of Jeremiah is to predict the downfall of God's people at the hands of the Babylonians. Not only will it predict the downfall, but also the restoration that God will bring in the end. He surely does have good plans for His people, as the key verse makes clear.

KEY VERSE

Jeremiah 29:10-11

The Weeping Prophet

SCRIPTURE READINGS

Day One: **Jeremiah 1-3**

Day Two: **Jeremiah 4-6**

Day Three: **Jeremiah 7-9**

Day Four: **Jeremiah 10-13**

Day Five: **Jeremiah 14-17**

Day Six: **Jeremiah 18-22**

Day Seven: **Jeremiah 23-25**

SUMMARIES

Day One: **Jeremiah 1-3**

We learn an interesting thing about how God works in these opening chapters of the Book of Jeremiah. It says that he was called to the ministry of prophecy from when he was in his mother's womb. This means that God doesn't wait to see what we will become before giving us a job in life. He has one for us at the very beginning before we are even born.

Day Two: **Jeremiah 4-6**

Disaster upon disaster strikes God's people for their lack of repentance. You'll see that the city of Jerusalem is highlighted along the way. Jerusalem is the capital city of Judah that was instituted by King David. If this city falls, the rest of the nation will tremble at its demise. This impending disaster strikes fear into God's people.

Day Three: **Jeremiah 7-9**

The fear of judgment is not enough to move God's people to action. Sin and wickedness run rampant in the land. So severe is the sin that Jeremiah earns his nickname in these verses. He says, "Oh that my head were waters, and my eyes a fountain of tears, that I might weep day and night for the slain of the daughter of my people."

Day Four: **Jeremiah 10-13**

The central issue among the different kinds of God's people is their allowance for idol worship in the nation. This is the issue at hand again, as Jeremiah calls out for reform among God's people. God is a jealous God who will not let another share in His glory. This is not pride or arrogance; this is simply right.

Day Five: **Jeremiah 14-17**

Jeremiah exemplifies for us a posture that we all ought to adopt. He recognizes the hopeless situation of God's people. He recognizes, too, that he can do nothing to change it. No amount of prophecy will change their hearts. The only One who can bring about change and salvation is God. And so, Jeremiah prays.

Day Six: **Jeremiah 18-22**

The imagery of the potter and the clay is powerful. God the Father is our potter. He has molded us in our mothers' wombs and created us for a unique purpose. How foolish it would be for the clay to demand anything of the potter. The clay only has value and purpose if the potter has His hands on it.

Day Seven: **Jeremiah 23-25**

Another word picture is painted for us in these chapters. Jesus must have read Jeremiah because He uses similar imagery in His own ministry. The picture of agriculture vineyards, in particular, would have been known to all who originally read and heard these prophecies. This would have clearly communicated that there are some good and some bad.

1. What do you think about the fact that God has a purpose for us before we are born?

2. What is God's purpose for your life?

3. Why is Jeremiah called the "weeping prophet?"

4. What good is it for Jeremiah to do such a miserable task?

5. How does the image of the potter and the clay help you understand God?

6. In what ways are we like the clay?

7. Who is the Righteous Branch that is foretold?

AUTHOR

Habakkuk

GENRE

Prophecy

PURPOSE

The Book of Habakkuk contains a prophecy concerning the captivity of God's people. As they suffer in chains and wonder at their plight, the prophet calls out on behalf of the people. He is racked with the question, "How long, O Lord?"

The interactions between Habakkuk and the Lord are as honest and genuine as they come. He brings honest frustrations and complains to God's lack of interference. And God graciously responds with the hard truth. God's people have earned their judgment. God refusing to intercede this time is a right punishment for wrong actions.

The purpose of the Book of Habakkuk is found in chapter 3. There, you will read a beautifully worded conclusion. I don't want to ruin that for you, so suffice it to say that Habakkuk resolves to trust the Lord, who is faithful to discipline and restoration.

KEY VERSE

Habakkuk 3:2

SCRIPTURE READINGS

Day One: **Jeremiah 26-29**

Day Two: **Jeremiah 30-31**

Day Three: **Jeremiah 32-34**

Day Four: **Jeremiah 35-37**

Day Five: **Jeremiah 38-40; Psalm 74, 79**

Day Six: **2 Kings 24-25; 2 Chronicles 36**

Day Seven: **Habakkuk 1-3**

SUMMARIES

Day One: **Jeremiah 26-29**

The struggle of Jeremiah is intensified during his ministry. He has to deal with false prophets in the midst of his prophetic ministry. It is hard enough to get God's people to believe and repent as it is. But to add false prophets along the way makes the task seem utterly impossible.

Day Two: **Jeremiah 30-31**

In these chapters, you find a crystal-clear picture of what Jesus came to accomplish. We have discussed the covenant of God with Abraham, Moses, and David. In these chapters, a new covenant is mentioned. Take these words in and hold onto them because Jesus will claim to inaugurate the new covenant during the Last Supper.

Day Three: **Jeremiah 32-34**

Jeremiah buys a field in the midst of the chaos. He doesn't do this because he is in desperate need of land. Nor does he have a building endeavor planned. No, he does this as a symbol of God's faithfulness. God will always own the land, no matter what nation occupies it. At any moment, God can return His people to the Promised Land.

Day Four: **Jeremiah 35-37**

As with other prophets, you'll see direct interactions with various kings along the way. In these chapters, Jeremiah will have run-ins with Zedekiah and Jehoiakim. Keep your finger marked in 2 Kings and 2 Chronicles to get the full picture of these interactions.

Day Five: **Jeremiah 38-40; Psalm 74, 79**

Another picture of God's plan in what happens to Jeremiah in these verses. Just as Jeremiah is cast into a pit, so will God's people be cast into the pit of captivity. And just as Jeremiah is rescued from the pit, so will God rescue His people from the pit. The Lord will deliver His helpless people.

Day Six: **2 Kings 24-25; 2 Chronicles 36**

What Jeremiah prophesied about firsthand, you can read about in the grand scheme in these chapters. Having these extra perspectives on the situation can help fill in some of the fuzzy details along the way. The point of these final chapters lines up with the point of Jeremiah. Judgment has come to God's people by the hand of Babylon.

Day Seven: **Habakkuk 1-3**

Habakkuk is a heart-wrenching and honest prophecy. You'll see the name Chaldeans. Don't let that confuse you. The name Chaldeans is essentially the same title for the Babylonians. The same plight that Jeremiah foretold is not being experienced by Habakkuk as he cries out to God.

1. Why would there be false prophets among God's people?

2. How can you tell a false prophet from a real one?

3. What kind of damage can a false prophet cause?

4. Which of the various word pictures helped you the most in your reading this week?

5. How could God deliver His people back to the Promised Land after all this?

6. What part of Habakkuk stood out to you the most?

7. Do you struggle to have the faith that Habakkuk expresses in Chapter 3?

AUTHOR

Jeremiah

GENRE

Prophecy

PURPOSE

The Book of Lamentations was written by the prophet Jeremiah during his prophetic ministry. It is a collection of songs that reflect funeral dirges. They are mournful and largely without hope, save a few select verses.

Each of these chapters contains one of the funeral dirges. They capture not only the reason for the troubles of God's people but also the incredible sorrow and suffering that accompanies it. Jeremiah is truly heartbroken over the state of God's people. Sadly, God's people are not nearly as sorrowful over their own sins.

The purpose of the Book of Lamentations is two-fold. The first reason is to capture glimpses of hope for God's people amidst incredible sorrow. The second reason is to teach us how to lament. There are times in our lives when the world is crumbling around us, and the best thing we can do is offer a prayer of lament to God.

KEY VERSE

Lamentations 3:22-23

Ezekiel

AUTHOR

Ezekiel

GENRE

Prophecy

PURPOSE

The prophetic book of Ezekiel is brilliant in its imagery. Pictures that can hardly be comprehended by the human mind are presented within its text. It can be mind-boggling, scary, and frustrating to wrap your mind around all that God had shown Ezekiel.

Be careful not to get too bogged down in what you can't picture that you miss what you can. The glory of the Lord leaves the temple. This shows Ezekiel that God has essentially left His people. Not forever, but for a moment in judgment. They have to reach rock bottom before they will realize their need for Him.

The purpose of the Book of Ezekiel is to show the great plan for God's people after the dust has settled. They will be judged by the nation of Babylon. They will endure the hardship of captivity. However, God's plan doesn't end there. There is a great restoration for a united kingdom of God.

KEY VERSE

Ezekiel 33:11

SCRIPTURE READINGS

Day One: **Jeremiah 41-45**
Day Two: **Jeremiah 46-48**
Day Three: **Jeremiah 49-50**
Day Four: **Jeremiah 51-52**
Day Five: **Lamentations 1-3:36**
Day Six: **Lamentations 3:37-5:22**
Day Seven: **Ezekiel 1-4**

SUMMARIES

Day One: **Jeremiah 41-45**

Unlike the vast majority of God's people, Jeremiah is taken to Egypt for captivity. He not only has to watch the devastation of God's land. And not only does one have to view the captivity of God's people as they are ushered to Babylone. He doesn't even get to go with them. He is completely helpless, aside from the great grace of God.

Day Two: **Jeremiah 46-48**

That God who allowed Jeremiah to be taken to Egypt and His people to Babylon has not overlooked their plight. Judgment is promised to them all and the surrounding nations. The Lord will put all things back into their proper place. Every wrong will be made right in the end by the great Judge of all creation.

Day Three: **Jeremiah 49-50**

The list of judgments continues in these chapters. Nation after nation is called out by God. No evil deed has gone unseen, and neither will they go unpunished. This ought to give us great hope as Christians. God says that vengeance belongs to Him, and He is faithful to provide justice at the right time.

Day Four: **Jeremiah 51-52**

Finally, Babylon, the great enemy of God's people, is named. Their judgment is sure. Their utter devastation is predicted. The great enemy will fall, and God will prevail. One day, God's people will be delivered. It's with that hope in mind that Jeremiah watches the temple burn. I can hear him utter, "Come quickly, Lord," as the ashes settle.

Day Five: **Lamentations 1-3:36**

Although it is Babylon who swings the sword and sets the fire, Jeremiah makes an important point in his laments. At the end of the day, it is God who sent Babylon to bring judgment. As angry as God's people want to be at the enemy, they must remember it is their own sin that God is judging. It's their fault this has happened.

Day Six: **Lamentations 3:37-5:22**

At the end of Jeremiah's ministry, he saw the Temple destroyed by the Babylonian armies. The rubble left over would have been overwhelming. Stones scattered everywhere. This is a picture of God's people at this time. Broken and scattered, they are holy stones that have been spread all over the place. Stones that only God can rebuild.

Day Seven: **Ezekiel 1-4**

While Jeremiah ends his time in Egypt, Ezekiel picks up the baton in Babylon. Living among God's exiled people, Ezekiel receives incredible visions of God's plan for His people. Sometimes, it can be helpful to try to draw some of the visions you read about. The images are so complex that it can be hard to build them in our minds without help.

1. How hard would it have been for Jeremiah to be separated from God's people?

2. How does hearing of God's judgment on His enemies inspire hope in His people?

3. Why doesn't God judge the enemies first?

4. What should God's people learn in their time of captivity?

5. Do you think the picture of scattered stones is accurate for God's people?

6. How do you think Jeremiah and Ezekiel would have interacted?

7. What kind of message do you expect from Ezekiel?

The Prophecy of Ezekiel

SCRIPTURE READINGS

Day One: **Ezekiel 5-8**
Day Two: **Ezekiel 9-12**
Day Three: **Ezekiel 13-15**
Day Four: **Ezekiel 16-17**
Day Five: **Ezekiel 18-19**
Day Six: **Ezekiel 20-21**
Day Seven: **Ezekiel 22-23**

SUMMARIES

Day One: **Ezekiel 5-8**

Jerusalem is not only the capital city of Judah; it is the home of the Temple. The Book of Ezekiel seems to center its focus around how God views the Temple. In these chapters, the incredible abominations that happen in and with the Temple are outlined for God's people. The judgment that is coming is justified.

Day Two: **Ezekiel 9-12**

The saddest moment in God's people's history is foretold in these chapters. The glory of the Lord is shown to Ezekiel as leaving the temple. Do you remember the massive celebration that took place when the Ark of the Covenant was carried into the temple? The glory of God was so overwhelming no one could stand it. Now it is gone, completely gone.

Day Three: **Ezekiel 13-15**

False prophets weren't just an issue for Jeremiah during this time period. But unlike Jeremiah, Ezekiel could go toe-to-toe with them. He was able to call them out directly and could likely talk with them face-to-face. They were undermining God's prophets, and this could not be tolerated.

Day Four: **Ezekiel 16-17**

We saw this imagery in Hosea, and we see it again now. God is like a faithful husband, and His people are like a faithless bride. They have spiritually cheated on Him by worshiping false idols and seeking refuge in foreign nations. They must remember the everlasting covenant that God made with them and come back to Him.

Day Five: **Ezekiel 18-19**

A sobering truth is taught in these chapters that we would all do well to remember. The soul who sins shall die. There is no escaping the just punishment for our sins. We deserve death with every white lie and blatant act of idolatry. No matter how big or small, every soul who sins shall die. This is why we so desperately need Jesus.

Day Six: **Ezekiel 20-21**

A terrifying image is shown in these chapters. The Lord draws His sword for the war that is to be waged. Jump ahead to the Book of Revelation, and you'll see that sword in the hand of His Son, Jesus. He wields it to judge and make war. The sword is a picture of the word of God that created all things now, bringing it to ruin.

Day Seven: **Ezekiel 22-23**

Israel is guilty of some detestable sins. However, it can be hard for us to remember that they breach even the most heinous of crimes. They are murderers. They cause unjust bloodshed to happen in their land. The leaders turn a blind eye to these actions and even participate in them when necessary (in their minds).

1. How does the Temple play a central role in Ezekiel?

2. What does it mean that the glory of God has left the temple?

3. Is there any hope for God's people if His glory has left?

4. What were some challenging images for you to understand in this book?

5. Did trying to draw them help you understand them?

6. What picture comes to mind when you hear of the Lord drawing a sword?

7. Is there a nation as corrupt today as Israel was then?

SCRIPTURE READINGS

Day One: **Ezekiel 24-27**

Day Two: **Ezekiel 28-31**

Day Three: **Ezekiel 32-34**

Day Four: **Ezekiel 35-37**

Day Five: **Ezekiel 38-39**

Day Six: **Ezekiel 40-41**

Day Seven: **Ezekiel 42-43**

SUMMARIES

Day One: **Ezekiel 24-27**

An interesting trend is forming in these chapters. It makes sense for Jeremiah to lament over God's people's enduring judgment because he is one of them. But Ezekiel, who is one of God's people, offers up multiple laments for those who are not a part of the kingdom of God. What compassion for the enemies of God!

Day Two: **Ezekiel 28-31**

Jeremiah is not safe in Egypt. The prophecy that comes from Ezekiel directs the aim towards Egypt and says that the Pharaoh will not survive the judgment. This will naturally send the nation into chaos and leave Jeremiah's life in the hands of whoever happens to be in charge at the time.

Day Three: **Ezekiel 32-34**

God holds the leadership of His people highly accountable for how poorly things are going for them. He uses shepherd language to drive home his point. The ones who ought to be leading and caring for the sheep are acting more like wolves. They are devouring their people to keep themselves satisfied.

Day Four: **Ezekiel 35-37**

I love the prophecy found in Chapter 37. Ezekiel goes to a valley of dry bones, a graveyard. And he is told to prophesy to the dead. Amazingly, God's breath fills the dead bones and clothes them with flesh again. What was once dead is made alive again. This is how God will save His people. The living Word will flow forth and raise dead men's souls.

Day Five: **Ezekiel 38-39**

There is a great war coming. One that will be more deadly and devastating than any war in history. It would be fair to call it an apocalyptic war. It'll be one to end all wars. At the end of this slaughter, the Lord will reign supreme. There will be no doubt that there is only One God in all the earth.

Day Six: **Ezekiel 40-41**

What grace! The Temple that was destroyed is now in sight. The Temple that the glory of God has left is pictured again. A new Temple is coming. A great Temple lies ahead for God's people. Ezekiel is undoubtedly trembling at the thought. Could God really restore them to such a point that their worship is pure again?

Day Seven: **Ezekiel 42-43**

Further and further into the vision of the new Temple, Ezekiel goes. With all the details of the original Temple under Solomon being revisited and revised, it's a beauty to behold. And then the wondrous, long-awaited event is seen. The glory of the Lord comes again to fill this place of worship. God will surely return to them!

1. Why would Ezekiel lament the destruction of foreign kingdoms?

2. How does the picture of the ravenous leaders of God's people make you feel?

3. Have you ever known a leader who devours his people for personal gain?

4. How can God hold leadership responsible for the sins of the nation?

5. What do you think the valley of dry bones means?

6. How does the vision of the new Temple compare to the other?

7. If the Lord doesn't return, is this new Temple worth looking forward to?

Joel

AUTHOR

Joel

GENRE

Prophecy

PURPOSE

Two great judgments befall God's people in the Book of Joel: a plague of locusts and a severe famine. Locusts are like giant grasshoppers that devour crops quickly. A plague of locusts would mean that the livelihood of the nation would be in jeopardy. Whatever survived the locusts were wiped out by the famine that hit the land.

Agriculturally speaking, it was the worst thing that could happen to God's people. Nationally, it caused a great crisis. Spiritually, it depicted the state of the nation. They were dry, desolate, and without fruit.

The point of the Book of Joel is to point God's people to fear the day of the Lord and return to Him before it is too late. If they will repent of their sins and return to God, He promises, as always, to restore them. The restoration will include all aspects of life: physical, spiritual, and national.

KEY VERSE

Joel 2:28

AUTHOR

Daniel

GENRE

Prophecy

PURPOSE

The Book of Daniel is half narrative and half prophecy. It contains some of the most note-worthy and memorable stories in all of the Bible. The running theme among God's men is their incredible boldness. Daniel and his friends stare death in the face many times and do not flinch.

Daniel is blessed by God along the way as an interpreter of dreams. Some of these dreams are wild, and it can be hard to understand their meaning. Graciously, God not only gives Daniel the meaning but it is recorded for us as well. Try not to make any guesses about what God does not reveal. We have all the information we need.

The purpose of the Book of Daniel is to show God's people that there is only One King whom they should fear. No matter how desperate their king becomes, there is a greater One to come. No matter how terrible the foreign king that holds them captive, their King is a mightier warrior.

KEY VERSE

Daniel 9:25-27

Bold Men of God

SCRIPTURE READINGS

Day One: **Ezekiel 44-45**
Day Two: **Ezekiel 46-48**
Day Three: **Joel 1-3**
Day Four: **Daniel 1-3**
Day Five: **Daniel 4-6**
Day Six: **Daniel 7-9**
Day Seven: **Daniel 10-12**

SUMMARIES

Day One: **Ezekiel 44-45**

The Temple is seen as being restored. The glory of God now dwells in it again. And the Levitical system is being reinstated. Nothing that was in God's original design is being overlooked. Ezekiel is witnessing a total restoration of the spiritual life of God's people. All they had lost in the Babylonian war will be returned to them.

Day Two: **Ezekiel 46-48**

What a beautiful city to behold. All that God's people need will be there for them. The Temple will be the center of life. Life itself will be flowing from its walls. The land will be divided again among God's people. But God's people will not be divided into two nations again.

Day Three: **Joel 1-3**

The devastation that is prophesied and experienced in the Book of Joel can be hard for us to wrap our minds around. If you don't have connections with agricultural life, it may not impact you the way it is intended to. Imagine a huge farm overwhelmed with ripe crops. Now imagine a swarm of large insects devouring it all. That is the devastation being experienced.

Day Four: **Daniel 1-3**

Daniel's interactions with the kings of Babylon begin with Nebuchadnezzar. He is not one to shy away from his beliefs. Instead of being thrown down for his strong beliefs, God blessed him. He allows Daniel to rise through the ranks of Babylon.

Day Five: **Daniel 4-6**

Nebuchadnezzar sees that there is a God greater than he. He offers up a song of praise that is genuine for the moment. But that recognition of God as supreme fads as time goes on. God does not let Nebuchadnezzar forget who He is. Sending message after message, the Lord makes it plain there will only be One King.

Day Six: **Daniel 7-9**

In these chapters begins the visions that Daniel receives. That is bizarre and hard to understand. Like with the dreams up to this point, we are given interpretations along the way. Resist the temptation to fill in any blanks that the Lord doesn't through His Word. There are things we are not meant to know.

Day Seven: **Daniel 10-12**

The Son of Man is a vision of Jesus, the coming greater King. Jesus Himself adopts this name in the Gospel according to Mark in the New Testament. This Son of Man will be sent by the Ancient of Days, which is an incredible name for God the Father. The Ancient One sends the Son of Man to save His people.

1. What does it say about God that He restores the Levitical system?

2. Why is the Temple the center of life in the new city?

3. Were you able to envision the locus and famine in Joel?

4. Which of the stories in Daniel stands out to you?

5. Why does God provide us with the interpretations of the dreams?

6. If you were the king, would you heed the writing on the wall?

7. How does reading about the Son of Man make you feel?

AUTHOR

Ezra

GENRE

History

PURPOSE

The Book of Ezra records, in part, the return of God's people from Babylon to their home, the Promised Land. There are all kinds of mixed emotions as this day draws near. Since God's people have been living in captivity for so long, Babylon now feels like their home. Israel feels like a distant memory.

Ezra works with God's people in making a plan to return. Part of the draw to stay in Babylon is that their former home is still in ruins. It will take years of work to restore the walls, the cities, and the Temple. Why leave an established life for a life of labor? Ezra wrestles with that question with God's people.

The purpose of the Book of Ezra is less about God's people's return and more about their faithful God. Throughout the prophetic books, God continues to promise restoration after the judgment. Now, restoration has come by His hand, and His people are hesitant to move forward.

KEY VERSE

Ezra 7:6

AUTHOR

Haggai

GENRE

Prophecy

PURPOSE

As God's people resettle in the Promised Land, everyone has different priorities. Some have focused on the rebuilding of the walls of the city. Some have dedicated their time to rebuilding their homes and their businesses. And a few were dedicated to rebuilding the Temple.

The Temple reconstruction started quickly. Within a short period of time, the foundation of the House of Worship was relaid. However, after the foundation is laid and worshiped around, it is forgotten. Years go by, and the Temple is still unfinished. But God's people did not stop working on their own homes.

The purpose of the Book of Haggai is to bring God's people to repentance. They have forgotten the God who delivered them back to the Promised Land. This is exemplified in the unfinished Temple. As the Lord says, "Is it a time for you yourselves to be living in your paneled houses while [the Temple] remains a ruin?"

KEY VERSE

Haggai 2:9

AUTHOR

Zechariah

GENRE

Prophecy

PURPOSE

The Old Testament sets its sights on the story of God's people and how God will save them from their sins. The overwhelming majority of the Old Testament points out Israel, the descendants of Abraham, the followers of Moses, and the kingdom under David, as the people of God.

The Book of Zechariah broadens the horizons of the reader to include a greater people to come. It teaches that all tribes of all nations will be given the chance of salvation. It echoes the idea found in Isaiah that says the Messiah will be a light to the Gentiles as well as the Jews. God's people are not bound by nationality or geography.

The purpose of the Book of Zechariah is to highlight one of the truths that undergirds the rest of the Old Testament. God's people are those who place their faith in the coming Messiah. For them, they awaited Jesus' first coming. For us, we await His return. Until then, salvation is available to all who would trust in Jesus.

KEY VERSE

Zechariah 13:9

Esther

Ezra

History

Some have questioned whether or not the Book of Esther ought to be included in the Bible because it does not contain a direct reference to God. His name is not recorded in any of the verses of this book of history. So why is it in the Bible?

There are a few reasons. The first is that it records a portion of the history of God's people. Esther becomes the Queen of Persia, who held God's people captive after Babylon. As one of God's people, she is put in a unique position that allows her to risk her own life for the sake of the rest of her nation. No spoilers will be found in this introduction, but it is an incredibly exciting story.

The second reason is that God's hand of providence is clearly in the story, even if it isn't explicitly stated. When you take all of the "coincidences" and risks necessary for the plan of Esther to work, you will quickly point to God as the only reason behind it all. The purpose of the Book of Esther is to show us that God is always at work, even if we don't see it happening.

Esther 4:14

God's People Return

SCRIPTURE READINGS

Day One: **Ezra 1-3**
Day Two: **Ezra 4-6; Psalm 137**
Day Three: **Haggai 1-2**
Day Four: **Zechariah 1-7**
Day Five: **Zechariah 8-14**
Day Six: **Esther 1-5**
Day Seven: **Esther 6-10**

SUMMARIES

Day One: **Ezra 1-3**

From one power to the next, God's people have been tossed around. First, the Assyrians had their fun with them. Then, the Babylonians carted them off. Finally, the Babylonians were conquered by the Persians, and God's people were the consolation promise. However, this change of power would turn out to be the reason God's people return home.

Day Two: **Ezra 4-6; Psalm 137**

A lot of history happens in these chapters. God's people return to the Promised Land. They see and assess the damage. They begin rebuilding, face struggles over that process and ultimately finish the rebuilding process. The story of Ezra centers on the rebuilding of the Temple, but so much more is happening around it.

Day Three: **Haggai 1-2**

Haggai is a prophecy smack dab in the middle of chapters 3 and 6 of Ezra. The people begin rebuilding the Temple, and then there is a great pause in the process. They finish their homes, but they forget about the house of God. Haggai calls them to repent over this issue.

Day Four: **Zechariah 1-7**

Vision after vision fills the mind and heart of Zechariah in his prophetic book. A key to understanding the visions is that God's people are not based on physical descendants but on faith. The measuring line for God's people is a spiritual one. The judgment and restoration belong to the people of faith within and outside of the nation of Israel.

Day Five: **Zechariah 8-14**

The Lord will give salvation to all who believe. To be clear, God will not save all people. Salvation is available to all but is not applied to all. It can only be received by grace through faith in the heart of any man. The Book of Zechariah makes this beautiful truth known to God's people in the nation of Israel.

Day Six: **Esther 1-5**

The story of Esther is a whirlwind drama. Esther's position and power in the kingdom of Persia seem to teeter and totter with the whims of the king. His unreliable emotional state makes every interaction with him a potentially volatile situation. How Esther navigates it all with the help of Mordecai is masterful.

Day Seven: **Esther 6-10**

The moment of utter irony has come. The enemy of God's people, Haman, had a set of gallows created for one of God's people, Mordecai. And yet it is Mordecai who is escorted on parade through the city. And it is Haman who is hanged on the gallows. God's ironic provision for His people is wonderful to read.

1. Why is Ezra's ministry focused on the Temple's reconstruction?

2. How did God use foreign kings to deliver His people home?

3. Why did some people weep when seeing the foundation of the Temple laid?

4. Is it fair for God to expect His home to be built before their homes?

5. What does God's desire to save all people reveal about His character?

6. What part of the story of Esther stood out to you?

7. Why do you think it is in the Bible?

AUTHOR

Malachi

GENRE

Prophecy

PURPOSE

Sadly, the reform and return of God's people from Babylon does not last forever. The final book of the Old Testament sets the tone for the 400 years of silence that exist between it and the New Testament. Malachi cries out to God's people to repent yet again. In comparison to God, who never changes, His people seem to change with the seasons.

Malachi's prophetic ministry looks ahead to the ministry of John the Baptist in the Gospel accounts of the New Testament. He foreshadows a coming servant of God that will prepare the way for the Messiah. Little do God's people know that this announcement will be followed by deafening silence for such a long time.

The purpose of the Book of Malachi is, sadly, the purpose of every prophet: to call God's people to repentance. Over and over again, they are in need of return and reform. In God's great grace, He offers these things to them every time. What a kind God we serve.

KEY VERSE

Malachi 3:6-7

AUTHOR

Luke

GENRE

Gospel Account

PURPOSE

Welcome to the New Testament! The Gospel, according to Luke, is not the first in the order of books, and it wasn't the first Gospel that was recorded. However, it does contain the earliest chronological story: the birth of John the Baptist.

What Malachi points forward to the Gospels answer. The one who was to come and prepare the way for the Messiah was John the Baptist. The Messiah who would come down the path laid by him was Jesus of Nazareth. In this Gospel account, you will get every detail of his birth, life, death, and resurrection.

The purpose of the Book of Luke is to record the life, death, and resurrection of Jesus with historical and scientific accuracy. This account was then given to Theophilus for his consideration. In turn, it has been given to us to consider who Jesus was and what He accomplished by His death on the cross.

KEY VERSE

Luke 4:18-21

John

John

Gospel Account

The Gospel, according to John, is the last to be written chronologically, but it contains more information concerning the ministry of John the Baptist, which is why you begin to read this book next.

The purpose of the Gospel, according to John, is said explicitly within his book. He says in John 20:30-31 ESV, "Now Jesus did many other signs in the presence of the disciples, which are not written in this book; but these are written so that you may believe that Jesus is the Christ, the Son of God and that by believing you may have life in his name."

The purpose of the Gospel, according to John, is so that whoever reads it will believe that Jesus is the Promised Savior of God's people and will believe that He is God. John records many accounts where Jesus claims deity indirectly. It would be impossible to read the account credibly and think of anything other than a divine assurance of Jesus.

John 3:16

God's People Rebuild

SCRIPTURE READINGS

Day One: **Ezra 7-10**
Day Two: **Nehemiah 1-5**
Day Three: **Nehemiah 6-7**
Day Four: **Nehemiah 8-10**
Day Five: **Nehemiah 11-13; Psalm 126**
Day Six: **Malachi 1-4**
Day Seven: **Luke 1; John 1:1-14**

SUMMARIES

Day One: **Ezra 7-10**

How Ezra goes about teaching God's Word is significant. We get many of our practices in the local church from this passage. They created a stage for the preacher. Something like a pulpit was built for the occasion. All people, regardless of age or gender, were invited to listen to the message. And Ezra explained the Scripture as he read it.

Day Two: **Nehemiah 1-5**

Ezra's focus in his ministry was on the rebuilding of the Temple. Nehemiah was focused on rebuilding the city walls and the city itself. Just as Ezra was given permission by a foreign king to return, so was Nehemiah. He was also given all the materials necessary to rebuild.

Day Three: **Nehemiah 6-7**

The lists of returned exiles can be difficult to read. You'll be tempted to skip right over it. However, I want you to take the time to read each name aloud. Each name is a person, not a number. Each name is a recipient of the grace of God. Each name was allowed to see the Promised Land again. This is not just any list. It's one that mirrors the Book of Life.

Day Four: **Nehemiah 8-10**

The worlds of Nehemiah and Ezra collide in these chapters. Reading these books in tandem with each other can bring a lot of additional understanding to the text. God is accomplishing two different but complementary goals through the leadership of these two people.

Day Five: **Nehemiah 11-13; Psalm 126**

God's people go through many reforms in the Old Testament. This is one of the last ones recorded in Scripture. They, like us, go through a constant cycle where reform and repentance are needed. The entire Christian life is going back and forth through the circle of belief and repentance until one day, we stand before our Savior.

Day Six: **Malachi 1-4**

Will God's people ever get it right? You would think after all they have been through and experienced, they would finally trust in God alone. It would make sense for the reformation to finally stick and hold true for generations to come. And yet, here they are again in need of repentance.

Day Seven: **Luke 1; John 1:1-14**

The long-awaited Messiah has come! Jesus is the greater Prophet promised to Moses. Jesus is the eternal King promised to David. Jesus is the reason for the entire Old Testament. He is the Word of God made into flesh. And by his sacrificed flesh, He will accomplish the great salvation that was promised way back in Genesis 3:15.

1. Does your local church teach God's Word like Ezra?

2. What lessons can we learn from how he taught God's people?

3. Is Nehemiah's focus on rebuilding the walls less significant than Ezra's goal?

4. What lessons can be learned from the life of Nehemiah?

5. How does reading the list of exiles with God's promise in mind change its meaning?

6. How do you feel ending the Old Testament on such a somber and sour note?

7. What role does John the Baptist play in redemptive history?

AUTHOR

Matthew

GENRE

Gospel Account

PURPOSE

The Gospel, according to Matthew, has some of the most extensive records of Jesus' teaching ministry. It contains well-known passages such as the Sermon on the Mount and the Olivet Discourse. Everything from the Beatitudes to the return of Christ is covered in this Gospel account.

One of the unique angels of Matthew is that he gives Old Testament proofs for much of what Jesus does. Your reading of the Old Testament will give you a lot of insight into what Matthew is trying to teach about Jesus' life, death, and resurrection.

Matthew has one great aim in his Gospel account. He is trying to prove beyond a shadow of a doubt that Jesus is the promised King that God told David about in His covenant. Matthew begins with a kingly lineage, shows a crown of thorns and robe on the way to the cross, and ends with victory over death in the resurrection.

KEY VERSE

Matthew 22:37-40

Mark

Gospel Account

The Gospel, according to Mark, is the shortest and most action-packed Gospel. Much less time is spent on Jesus' teachings in comparison to the actions and stories surrounding Jesus' life. You'll see terms like "immediately" and "after that" used many times. Mark pushes the story forward to the main event: the death and resurrection of Jesus.

One unique thing to note about the Gospel, according to Mark, is the use of the term "Son of Man" in reference to Jesus. Do you remember this term from the Book of Daniel? In it, the Son of Man was the warrior King that the Ancient of Days was sending to save His people. In the Gospel, according to Mark, Jesus is the Son of Man, but He doesn't come as He expected.

The purpose of the Gospel of Mark is to show that this man, Jesus, was more than just a man. He was God made flesh. He was the Son of Man and the savior of the world. Every reader of Mark should walk away amazed at the miraculous power that confirmed the message of Jesus: "For even the Son of Man did not come to be served, but to serve, and to give His life as a ransom for many."

Mark 10:45

The Gospel Accounts

SCRIPTURE READINGS

Day One: **Matthew 1; Luke 2:1-38**
Day Two: **Matthew 2; Luke 2:39-52**
Day Three: **Matthew 3; Mark 1; Luke 3**
Day Four: **Matthew 4; Luke 4-5; John 1:15-51**
Day Five: **John 2-4**
Day Six: **Mark 2**
Day Seven: **John 5**

SUMMARIES

Day One: **Matthew 1; Luke 2:1-38**

These chapters focus on the miraculous birth of Jesus. One thing that is highlighted about Jesus' birth is that He was born of a virgin. The importance of this cannot be overstated. If Jesus is born like any other child, he will inherit from Adam the curse of sin. Since He was born supernaturally, He is like a second Adam who can redeem the fall of the first.

Day Two: **Matthew 2; Luke 2:39-52**

Very little is known about Jesus' life before the age of 30, when His ministry formally began. What we do know is found in these chapters. He was an ordinary child in that he needed his parents to guide him. He had health concerns. And He had to eat and drink. But He was unique in how people viewed Him and listened to Him.

Day Three: **Matthew 3; Mark 1; Luke 3**

John the Baptist is the forerunner of Jesus. As Jesus was growing older and before the beginning of His official ministry, John the Baptist was already hard at work. He was preaching and teaching the message of Malachi: repent and believe. Those who would repent were baptized by full immersion into water. Jesus, to fulfill all righteousness, was baptized by John. And thus began His ministry.

Day Four: **Matthew 4; Luke 4-5; John 1:15-51**

Immediately after His baptism, Jesus is tempted into the wilderness. Think back to how God's people came through the waters of the Red Sea and were tempted into the wilderness. Jesus is now being tempted in the greatest ways possible. However, Jesus does not make the mistake of Israel or repeat the sin of Adam. He remains faithful.

Day Five: **John 2-4**

John 2 contains Jesus' earliest recorded miracles. At the wedding He was attending, He did the impossible and turned water into well-aged wine. Just by the sound of His voice, creation obeyed His command to become something new. Jesus, from the very beginning of His ministry, was proving Himself to be God.

Day Six: **Mark 2**

After His first miracle, the excitement around Jesus builds and builds. People are beginning to follow Him. They are coming to expect to see miracles when He is around. In these chapters, Jesus begins to assert Himself as a healer, an authoritative teacher, and someone worth following. Those who do formally follow Him are called His disciples.

Day Seven: **John 5**

In these chapters, Jesus makes the claim to be equal to God, the Father. The religious leaders of the day were unsure of what to do about Jesus, but He hadn't really caused any trouble. That was until He began to claim to be God. They had to put an end to His ministry, which ultimately meant an end to His life.

1. Why is it important that Jesus was born of a virgin?

2. Was there anything special about Mary for her to be chosen for this task?

3. How do you think Joseph felt about Mary's pregnancy?

4. Why was it necessary for Jesus to be baptized?

5. Which of Jesus' miracles so far has stood out to you?

6. Why would Jesus claiming to be God make the religious leaders mad?

7. Has anyone made a claim that has made you uncomfortable?

The Teachings of Christ

SCRIPTURE READINGS

Day One: **Matthew 12:1-21; Mark 3; Luke 6**
Day Two: Matthew 5-7
Day Three: Matthew 8:1-13; Luke 7
Day Four: Matthew 11
Day Five: Matthew 12:22-50; Luke 11
Day Six: Matthew 13; Luke 8
Day Seven: Matthew 8:14-34; Mark 4-5

SUMMARIES

Day One: **Matthew 12:1-21; Mark 3; Luke 6**

Jesus claims to be Lord over the Sabbath. This would have been an impossible thing for the religious leaders to hear. They had their own rules and interpretations of what honoring the Sabbath looked like. For Jesus to actively break their rules and regulations naturally upset them. Worse yet, Jesus was establishing Himself as the new standard for what is God's Law.

Day Two: **Matthew 5-7**

These chapters are often called the Sermon on the Mount for obvious reasons. It all takes place on the mountainside. As you'll read, it begins as a small teaching moment between Jesus and His twelve disciples. Somewhere along the way, a massive crowd grows, as you'll see in the ending verses and following chapters.

Day Three: **Matthew 8:1-13; Luke 7**

In Luke 7, Jesus does something that ought to ring in your ears. He raises the son of a widow. Both Elijah and Elisha, the great prophets of the Old Testament, ministered to widows in this way. If there was any doubt, it has been removed. Jesus is just as much a prophet as the ones of the Old Testament.

Day Four: **Matthew 11**

Jesus has God-like compassion for the people that He interacts with. Just like the Father would send messages of judgment as well as messages of restoration, Jesus proclaims both. They are both true of our life before God. He will not overlook any sin, but we have salvation from our sin by grace through faith in Jesus.

Day Five: **Matthew 12:22-50; Luke 11**

These chapters contain one of the most debated verses in the Bible. The one concerning blasphemy of the Holy Spirit. It is often called the unpardonable sin. What does all of this mean? It means that if you reject the Holy Spirit and harden your heart, you will not be forgiven of your sins. How could you if salvation only comes by responding to the Holy Spirit in faith?

Day Six: **Matthew 13; Luke 8**

Just like the dreams in Joseph's life and in Daniel's life, the parables of Jesus often come with explanations. This made life for the disciples and life for us much easier. We do not have to guess at what Jesus meant. He tells us plainly in these helpful chapters about the kingdom of God.

Day Seven: **Matthew 8:14-34; Mark 4-5**

You'll have noticed by now that you're jumping around a lot. Not only between Gospel accounts, but you're also jumping around within certain books. This is because each Gospel account records the events of Jesus' life in a different order. This doesn't make one right or wrong. It just adds to the unique perspective and ultimate goal of the writing itself.

1. Why does Jesus have the right to be Lord over the Sabbath?

2. What man-made rules about religion exist today?

3. In what ways is Jesus a greater prophet than Elijah or Elisha?

4. Which of Jesus' parables was the hardest for you to understand?

5. Were there any parables that you still don't understand, even with the following explanation?

6. How does reading various accounts of the same event help you understand them?

Which Gospel writer do you enjoy reading the most?

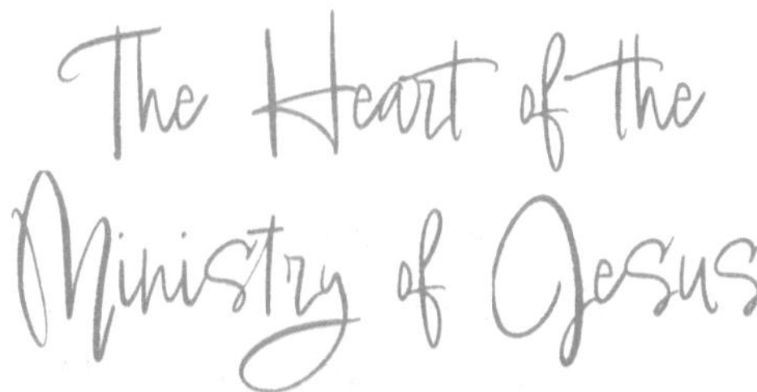

The Heart of the Ministry of Jesus

SCRIPTURE READINGS

Day One: **Matthew 9-10**
Day Two: **Matthew 14; Mark 6; Luke 9:1-17**
Day Three: **John 6**
Day Four: **Matthew 15; Mark 7**
Day Five: **Matthew 16; Mark 8; Luke 9:18-27**
Day Six: **Matthew 17; Mark 9; Luke 9:28-62**
Day Seven: **Matthew 18**

SUMMARIES

Day One: **Matthew 9-10**

In these chapters, Jesus finishes His selection of His disciples. It should catch your eye that there are 12 disciples chosen. The reason this is significant is because there were 12 tribes of Israel. Jesus is establishing a new kind of people under a new covenant yet to be revealed.

Day Two: **Matthew 14; Mark 6; Luke 9:1-17**

The death of John the Baptist is a sad moment in redemptive history. His role in the life and ministry of Jesus is not a small one. He prepared the way for Jesus. He served alongside Jesus. He was Jesus' own flesh and blood. The passing of John was sure to make an impact on Jesus and His disciples.

Day Three: **John 6**

This chapter contains the first of the "I am" statements of Christ. He makes an analogy about Himself in various passages, and in this one, He likens Himself to the Bread of Life. His meaning is looking back to the wilderness journey of Israel with Moses. God provided bread from heaven to save their physical life. Jesus was born from heaven to save our spiritual lives.

Day Four: **Matthew 15; Mark 7**

Along the way in Jesus' ministry, you'll see Him begin to branch out to other nations and people of various faiths. He takes His gospel message to Gentiles as well as the Jews. In sad irony, the most response He receives is not from God's people in the Jews, but from God's people in the Gentiles.

Day Five: **Matthew 16; Mark 8; Luke 9:18-27**

The religious leaders called the Pharisees and Sadusees, cannot stand the ministry of Jesus by this point. He has grown far past a nuisance. They need to get rid of Him, and so they begin to challenge Him at every point. They try to trick Him by asking impossible questions and demanding signs. Yet Jesus has the perfect answer every time.

Day Six: **Matthew 17; Mark 9; Luke 9:28-62**

The transfiguration of Jesus is a remarkable event that only 3 of the 12 disciples got to witness. These 3 are often called the inner circle of Jesus' disciples. There, on the mountain, Jesus met with Moses (a representation of the Law of God) and Elijah (a representation of the prophets of God). After all was done, only One Man remained, the fulfillment of the Law and Prophets, Jesus.

Day Seven: **Matthew 18**

Jesus taught heavily against sin. He warned His followers of its dangers and encouraged them to not let sinful situations go unresolved. In Matthew 18, the blueprint for lovingly bringing someone to repentance is given to us. It is a process that is sadly neglected in the church but very much needed.

1. What do you notice about the differences in the 12 disciples?

2. Why is it important for Jesus to choose 12 different kinds of men?

3. What does Jesus mean when He says, "I am the Bread of Life?"

4. What tactics do the religious leaders use to shut down Jesus?

5. Why are they unable to outsmart Him?

6. Why won't they follow Him?

7. Have you used the Matthew 18 method to bring someone to repentance?

The Parables of Jesus

SCRIPTURE READINGS

Day One: **John 7-8**
Day Two: **John 9:1-41; John 10:1-21**
Day Three: **Luke 10-11; John 10:22-42**
Day Four: **Luke 12-13**
Day Five: **Luke 14-15**
Day Six: **Luke 16; Luke 17:1-10**
Day Seven: **John 11**

SUMMARIES

Day One: **John 7-8**

"I am the Light of the World" is another one of the famous "I am" statements of Christ. This theme of Jesus being the light in a dark world runs all the way through the Gospel, according to John. It begins in the opening chapter and ends when the sky turns black at His crucifixion.

Day Two: **John 9:1-10:21**

"I am the Good Shepherd" is a powerful phrase in the ears of Jesus' listeners. Shepherds play an important part in the history of God's people. Abraham, Moses, and David were all shepherds. The corrupt leaders of God's people were called ravenous shepherds. And now Jesus claims the title of Good Shepherd.

Day Three: **Luke 10-11; John 10:22-42**

The religious leaders are so amazed and frustrated by the ministry of Jesus that they resort to illogical lies to bring Him down. They claim that the power He is using to perform all of His miracles comes from

"Beelzebub," which is another name for the Devil. But why would the Devil drive out his own demons? It is a power only of God.

Day Four: **Luke 12-13**

So far in Jesus' ministry, He hasn't been too forceful with the religious leaders. However, after this last interaction, He makes His views plain. He refers to the Pharisees as leaven. Leaven is the product used in bread to make it rise. It only takes a little bit for the whole loaf to be affected. In this way, Jesus says to beware of these religious leaders.

Day Five: **Luke 14-15**

These chapters contain three of the most powerful and memorable parables of Jesus. Each one contains something lost: a sheep, a coin, and a son. At first glance, it may seem that those lost things are the main point of the parable. But the main point is the main character: the shepherd, the woman, and the Father. Read them in light of that.

Day Six: **Luke 16; Luke 17:1-10**

The parable of the rich man and Lazarus is unique in two ways. The first is that it is the only parable where a character has an actual name. The second is that it is a vision of what Heaven and Hell are like. Since it is a parable, it is not meant to be an exact representation, but there are valuable lessons to learn from it.

Day Seven: **John 11**

Another Lazarus is mentioned in this story. Perhaps Jesus was inspired by his good friend when teaching the parable of yesterday. Jesus mourns the loss of His friend and the pain His other friends feel. However, He does not leave the situation as it is. He raises Lazarus from the grave.

1. What does it mean that Jesus is the Light of the World?

2. Why is Jesus' title as Good Shepherd so impactful?

3. Which of the parables of Jesus stood out to you this week?

4. What is the significance of the older brother in the Lost/ Prodigal Son story?

5. What did you learn about Heaven in Jesus' parable of Lazarus?

6. What did you learn about Hell in Jesus' parable of Lazarus?

7. When Jesus wept, how does that reveal Hs humanity?

The Triumphal Entry

SCRIPTURE READINGS

Day One: **Luke 17:11-37; Luke 18:1-14**
Day Two: **Matthew 19; Mark 10**
Day Three: **Matthew 20-21**
Day Four: **Luke 18:15-19:48**
Day Five: **Mark 11; John 12**
Day Six: **Matthew 22; Mark 12**
Day Seven: **Matthew 23; Luke 20-21**

SUMMARIES

Day One: **Luke 17:11-37; Luke 18:1-14**

Jesus' parable of the persistent widow gives us a lot of hope as Christians. In this parable, the widow never stops asking for what she needs. She essentially wears the other person down until they give in. Consider your relationship with God. We have nowhere to wear Him down. We may need to be persistent, but He will always give us the best thing for us in the end.

Day Two: **Matthew 19; Mark 10**

Jesus' teaching on divorce is important for us to note. In our world today, divorce is a common reality in most families. Jesus teaches two main things about divorce. First is that it is not God's desire for anyone to get divorced. The second is that while God doesn't desire it, He allows it for specific reasons.

Day Three: **Matthew 20-21**

The Triumphal Entry of Jesus is a monumental moment in His ministry. From this point forward, He will not travel. In just a week, He will be tried, condemned, and crucified. His whole demeanor changes as He rides into the city. His face is set in stone, and He is determined to accomplish the mission He came to earth for to save sinners like us.

Day Four: **Luke 18:15-19:48**

I love the story of Jesus and Zacchaeus. Not only do I relate to Zacchaeus because I am short, but I am amazed at the intentionality of Jesus. He stops in the middle of His walk through town. He overlooks the crowds to find Zacchaeus in the trees. He has dinner with the hated man. And He shows the same love and care He has for His disciples, to him.

Day Five: **Mark 11; John 12**

A precious moment is recorded here. Mary has very little to her name. Her reputation in the community is tarnished because of her past. So when she enters the room where Jesus and some others recline, the conversation comes to a halt. Jesus does not turn her away. He welcomes her, and she blesses Him with a special gift.

Day Six: **Matthew 22; Mark 12**

When Jesus says, "Give to Caesar what is Caesar's," He makes a very clear statement on how the Christian should live in the world. We ought to live with respect for our government. This does not mean we have to agree with everything the government does. It does mean we don't have the right to pursue anarchy.

Day Seven: **Matthew 23; Luke 20-21**

Jesus' anger towards the religious leaders is never without compassion. The "woes" that He has for them are because of His genuine sorrow for where they stand. They will be judged for how they are trying to lead those around them. They will find themselves in the opposite position except for rejecting Jesus as Lord.

1. What does your prayer life look like?

2. Are there things you ought to be more persistent in prayer over?

3. How do you understand Jesus' teachings on divorce?

4. Are there other reasons the Bible says divorce is permissible?

5. How do people go from shouting "Hosanna" to "Crucify Him" so quickly?

6. What is the significance of Mary's gift to Jesus?

7. How are we to live under our governments?

The Return of Christ

SCRIPTURE READINGS

Day One: Mark 13

Day Two: Matthew 24

Day Three: Matthew 25

Day Four: Matthew 26; Mark 14

Day Five: Luke 22; John 13

Day Six: John 14-17

Day Seven: Matthew 27; Mark 15

SUMMARIES

Day One: Mark 13

The destruction of the Temple, as you can imagine by now, is a sore spot for God's people. They have seen and rebuilt and mourned over this many times. So, for Jesus to proclaim that He could destroy and rebuild the Temple in three days was insulting to the listeners. What they didn't understand is that He was referring to His own body as the dwelling place of God.

Day Two: Matthew 24

A heavy question in the minds and hearts of Jesus' followers is when the end of time would come. They were all expecting the Messiah to be a military leader that would give them back their sovereignty as a nation. Jesus hadn't done anything resembling that, and so the question bubbled up in their conversation.

Day Three: Matthew 25

Jesus gives not only the signs to look for in the end, but He explains what preparation for the end looks like. After Jesus' death and resurrection, He will return as the Messiah they were expecting. He will return as a conquering King and will set up His reign among all people. Until then, His disciples were to prepare for that day.

Day Four: **Matthew 26; Mark 14**

The time has finally come. Jesus' adversaries are making plans for His execution. The religious leaders have had enough, and they can think of no other way to silence Jesus and His followers. And so they begin to plot and scheme. Ultimately, they find their answer in one of Jesus' disciples, who is willing to betray Him.

Day Five: **Luke 22; John 13**

This betrayal of Jesus from Judas did not come as a shock to Him. It was all necessary to fulfill the ultimate plan of dying on the cross for the sins of the world. Although it was expected, it hurt nonetheless. Spending three years caring for and leading a person only to have them sell you out for the price of a slave is deeply painful.

Day Six: **John 14-17**

After the Last Supper and the betrayal of Jesus is set into motion, He shares final words with His disciples. This would be the last major teaching time in His ministry. It is not reserved for the crowds at large but for His (now 11) disciples. He gives them hope to hold onto in the midst of the coming trial.

Day Seven: **Matthew 27; Mark 15**

The saddest day in human history. The Son of God was crucified on the cross. An innocent man was put to death. Jesus, the savior of the world, hung lifeless on a tree. The disciples weep and scatter. In utter fear and confusion, they are unsure of what is to happen next.

1. Why is the destruction of the temple a sore spot for the religious leaders?

2. What did Jesus mean when He said He could build it in 3 days?

3. What signs did you not expect to read about the end times?

4. Have you seen any of these signs already?

5. In what ways can you prepare for the return of Jesus?

6. What of Jesus' crucifixion stands out to you?

7. What hope do the disciples have now that Jesus has died?

Acts

AUTHOR

Luke

GENRE

History

PURPOSE

The Book of Acts has been given different names throughout history. Some people call it the Book of the Acts of the Apostles or Disciples. This is because it traces what the disciples did after the resurrection and ascension of Jesus. It describes how the church was formed and began to grow.

Some people call it the Book of the Acts of the Holy Spirit. Where the Father was the major actor in the Old Testament and the Son the major actor in the Gospels, now the Holy Spirit takes a large role in forming the church and setting it into motion.

Whatever title you give it, the same ultimate purpose remains. The purpose of the Book of Acts is to show the beginning of the Church, the Bride of Christ for whom He died. The struggles, the experience, and the growth that follows are nothing short of a miraculous work of God.

KEY VERSE

Acts 1:8

The Resurrection of Jesus

SCRIPTURE READINGS

Day One: Luke 23; John 18-19
Day Two: Matthew 28; Mark 16
Day Three: Luke 24; John 20-21
Day Four: Acts 1-3
Day Five: Acts 4-6
Day Six: Acts 7-8
Day Seven: Acts 9-10

SUMMARIES

Day One: Luke 23; John 18-19

In these two Gospel accounts, you'll find the most detailed views of the crucifixion. Luke, being a physician by trade, gives the most vivid details of them all. It is heart-wrenching to read, but it is good to read. It shows us the reality of the death of Jesus and provides historical accuracy so that we can trust what we're reading to be true.

Day Two: Matthew 28; Mark 16

If the crucifixion is the darkest day in history, then the resurrection of Jesus is the greatest day. Three days of wandering, fear, and silence were broken on that Sunday morning. Each Gospel account recalls various people going to see the empty tomb. Each time, those individuals rushed back to tell the rest of the disciples.

Day Three: Luke 24; John 20-21

Jesus appeared to many disciples after His resurrection. No longer bound by a typical human body, Jesus was able to appear where He wanted. It's striking that Jesus appeared not to the 12 disciples first but to influential women in His life. He gave them precedence when He could have gone to the inner circle.

Day Four: **Acts 1-3**

After the ascension of Jesus, the disciples waited for the promised gift of the Holy Spirit. When He came down and filled the disciples with His power, the Church was born. Thousands were added to the Church on the Day of Pentecost. From there, this movement of God spread throughout Jerusalem.

Day Five: **Acts 4-6**

Peter, the one who denied Jesus, now stood boldly before the religious leaders to proclaim His great name. The disciples, now referred to as the apostles, endured many hardships. They were imprisoned for their faith, but the Lord was faithful to deliver them. These once-timid followers of Jesus were impassioned and empowered by what they had experienced.

Day Six: **Acts 7-8**

After the first recorded Christian martyrdom, it is one of the enemies of the Church. A man named Saul was zealous for his religious beliefs and made it his mission to dismantle the Church. But despite his efforts, they continued to grow and prosper.

Day Seven: **Acts 9-10**

Acts 9 records an incredible event in church history. The enemy, Saul, was converted to Christianity. After an incredible experience on the road to Damascus, Saul gave his life to follow and proclaim Jesus as Lord. Saul would later be named Paul, the man who wrote the majority of the books of the New Testament.

1. How did Luke and John's accounts of the crucifixion differ from Matthew and Mark's?

2. What stood out to you about the resurrection?

3. Why do you think Jesus visited the women before the disciples?

4. What do you think the Day of Pentecost would have looked like?

5. Have you ever experienced someone speaking in tongues like that?

6. How does Stephen's death inspire you to follow Jesus?

7. Do you have a Damascus Road moment like Saul?

AUTHOR

James

GENRE

Epistle

PURPOSE

The Book of James is written to the scattered people of God. As you'll read in the Book of Acts, the Church undergoes severe persecution. This persecution forces them to scatter all over the area. James writes this letter, and it is meant to be passed around from church to church.

One of the main ideas of James' letter is that faith must be accompanied by works. The thought goes like this: if you really believe something to be true, then your life will reflect that belief. If you believe a chair can bear your weight, then you'll sit in it. James says that faith without works is dead.

The purpose of the Book of James is to explain what a life of faith looks like. He is less concerned with espousing deep and profound theology. His goal is to talk about what a Christian ought to live like if his faith is genuine.

KEY VERSE

James 2:26

AUTHOR

Paul

GENRE

Epistle

PURPOSE

There is an issue among the people in the church of Galatia. They are arguing over whether or not non-Jewish Christians ought to be circumcised. Think back to how God's people began. The sign of the covenant that was given to Abraham was circumcision. If you were a part of God's people, then this would be done to you.

So when non-Jewish people started believing in Jesus for salvation, the Jews were tempted to say that they must be circumcised. Paul addresses this issue head-on in his letter to the Galatians. He refutes that idea and says that adding any good work to faith for salvation nullifies the grace that faith brings.

Paul and James are saying the same thing from different angles. Both are saying that we are saved by grace alone through faith alone. And both would say that saving faith never comes alone. Good works are a result of saving faith. They do not earn it. Explaining this idea is the purpose of the Book of Galatians.

KEY VERSE

Galatians 2:16

The Spread of the Gospel

SCRIPTURE READINGS

Day One: **Acts 11-12**
Day Two: **Acts 13-14**
Day Three: **James 1-5**
Day Four: **Acts 15-16**
Day Five: **Galatians 1-3**
Day Six: **Galatians 4-6**
Day Seven: **Acts 17; Acts 18:1-18**

SUMMARIES

Day One: **Acts 11-12**

As the Church spread due to persecution, so does the Gospel message. Because of this, many different people from many different backgrounds become believers. This makes the church worship services very interesting because these people wouldn't normally associate. Peter and Paul help these new churches navigate the new life they now live.

Day Two: **Acts 13-14**

After being trained for a few years, Paul became a missionary and church planter. Much of the rest of the Book of Acts is dedicated to telling of Paul's missionary journeys and the different churches he helped begin. As you read his letters in the New Testament, you'll learn more about the ministry he provided there.

Day Three: **James 1-5**

James' letter is a pivotal one in the life of the church. It is very easy for someone to say they have faith but never act on it. James' ultimate point is that true faith is never without good works. People of genuine Christian faith will seek to control their speech, not show favoritism, care for orphans and widows, and many more things.

Day Four: **Acts 15-16**

Paul's split from Barnabas opens the door for him to meet and work with Timothy. You'll notice his name as you read the rest of the New Testament. Paul writes two letters specifically to him. Paul becomes his mentor and heavily influences the kind of pastor and preacher Timothy will become.

Day Five: **Galatians 1-3**

The first half of the Book of Galatians deals with the issue of circumcision. Paul makes it clear that while he has deep Jewish roots, the Gospel does not demand circumcision for salvation. If we add anything to the work of Jesus for our salvation, then we nullify the need for His sacrifice.

Day Six: **Galatians 4-6**

The second half of the book of Galatians puts the first half into practice. If we really are saved by faith alone, then that drastically changes how we live our lives. It causes us to bear one another's burdens. It compels us to put on the armor of God. It means that our faith in Jesus gives us freedom to live a life honoring God.

Day Seven: **Acts 17:1-18:18**

Paul rapidly travels around the area. He is passionate about taking the Gospel to the ends of the earth. His ultimate aim is to take it to Rome. God guides his steps and doesn't allow him to go straight there. There is much work for him to do before he takes that long journey.

1. Do you think it was a good thing that the Church was persecuted?

2. How do you navigate going to church with people of different backgrounds?

3. What lesson in James' letter is the hardest struggle for you?

4. Do you agree that faith without works is dead?

5. Why is it okay for Paul and Barnabas to split?

6. Have you ever had a mentor like Timothy did with Paul?

7. Who is someone that you could be a spiritual mentor for?

AUTHOR

Paul

GENRE

Epistle

PURPOSE

Paul did not plant a church and leave it to fend for itself. He kept up with them by sending letters back and forth. We have many letters that he sent recorded in Scripture, and they beat the names of the churches they were sent to.

The Book of 1 Thessalonians gives great insight to the Christian who is concerned with the return of Jesus. It answers the questions that surround what will happen to those who die before He returns. The particular concern is what will happen to their bodies.

When Jesus resurrected, He had a glorified body. When He comes back, he will give us glorified bodies like His. But what happens to those who have died before His return. What will become of their bodies that have decayed or even been cremated and scattered? The answers are found in this book.

KEY VERSE

1 Thessalonians 4:14-17

2 Thessalonians

AUTHOR

Paul

GENRE

Epistle

PURPOSE

The second letter to the church in Thessalonica has similar concerns to the first. The questions are still wrapped up in how things will end. If you can remember reading about the day of the lord, they are having questions about how that will look.

Many of them have stopped working because they feel the Day of the Lord is coming close. So, instead of working, they are simply watching and waiting for the Lord to return. Paul corrects that thinking and encourages him to continue in their work and watch while they are working.

The purpose of the book of 2 Thessalonians is to push Christians forward even when they face persecution. There will be times when we will feel like giving up and throwing in the towel. But until Jesus returns, we still have a job to do. We must get to work.

KEY VERSE

2 Thessalonians 3:3

AUTHOR

Paul

GENRE

Epistle

PURPOSE

The church that Paul planted in the city of Corinth quickly became a Church full of problems. After he left, they lost their way. They forgot the truth of the gospel and their need for Jesus.

Paul has to handle issues like divisions in the church, sexual immorality, and the misuse of spiritual gifts. In this letter, he is very direct because the cost of being wrong is so high. He is not happy to see one of his churches go astray.

The purpose of the Book of 1 Corinthians is to remind the Church of the need for spiritual purity. If any local church goes astray, spiritually, they will only do damage and not serve the purpose they were created for. They were created to share the good news with the world and make disciples of all nations.

KEY VERSE

1 Corinthians 15:3-4

SCRIPTURE READINGS

Day One: 1 Thessalonians 1-5; 2 Thessalonians 1-3
Day Two: Acts 18:19-28; Acts 19:1-41
Day Three: 1 Corinthians 1-4
Day Four: 1 Corinthians 5-8
Day Five: 1 Corinthians 9-11
Day Six: 1 Corinthians 12-14
Day Seven: 1 Corinthians 15-16

SUMMARIES

Day One: 1 Thessalonians 1-5; 2 Thessalonians 1-3

The letters written to the church and Thessalonica are both concerning the end times. They have questions about how Jesus' return will impact the dead and what the awesome day of the Lord will be like. Paul calms their concerns and gives them comfort. If you are interested in the end, then these letters will be a big help to you.

Day Two: Acts 18:19-28; Acts 19:1-41

You will be back in the Book of Acts today. As you read through the stories about Paul's missionary journeys, you will learn more and more about the churches that Paul is writing to in his letters. Take note of how Paul's initial work in Corinth begins and prepare yourself for the letter. He sent it to them a few years later.

Day Three: 1 Corinthians 1-4

At the church that Paul planted in, Corinth now has some major issues. There are divisions in the church, and people are picking sides under various leaders. While each of the leaders is a godly man, their following has become an issue.

Day Four: **1 Corinthians 5-8**

The divisions that exist in the church are the least of the problems within the church. There are issues of sexual immorality. There are lawsuits happening among the believers. And there are all kinds of marital problems that they are working through. This truly was an imperfect church.

Day Five: **1 Corinthians 9-11**

The point that Paul makes in these chapters is an incredible one for us to behold. Paul often gives up his own rights to certain things for the sake of his brothers and sisters. If he knows that what he is free to do will cause another person to stumble. In their faith, he will refrain from doing that thing.

Day Six: **1 Corinthians 12-14**

These chapters that Paul writes to the church in Corinth are all about spiritual gifts. There are many gifts that seem to have ceased today. Although we cannot know that for sure, we can be sure that there are some that are still active. Gifts of teaching, encouragement, and the like are all very relevant to the church today.

Day Seven: **1 Corinthians 15-16**

These final chapters from Paul are all about the resurrection of Jesus. Some of the members of the church in Corinth are struggling to accept and understand the reality of resurrection. But Paul points to the scripture as proof enough to believe that Jesus is alive today.

1. What questions do you have about the end times?

2. What do you think it will be like when we are caught up in the air with Jesus?

3. Have you ever experienced the pain of a divided church?

4. What kind of moral issues exist in the church that you attend?

5. How can you learn to give up your own rights like Paul did?

6. What are some of your spiritual gifts?

7. Do you ever question the reality of the resurrection?

AUTHOR

Paul

GENRE

Epistle

PURPOSE

The second letter to the church in Corinth celebrates the original letter was received well. That he'll his warnings and took his advice. They had made Strauss towards unity and holiness. But there was still work to be done.

A group of false teachers had arisen up in the church. They had begun to attack Paul's character and even his speech problems. Paul pushed back with the simplicity of the gospel. On top of the false teachers, there were still plenty of members of the church who were living in sin. Paul addressed those things as well.

The purpose of the book of Second Corinthians is to remind the believer that the pursuit of holiness is never finished. Even when a church has made significant progress, there will always be room to grow. Until Jesus comes back, nothing, not even the church, will be perfect.

KEY VERSE

2 Corinthians 5:17

Romans

AUTHOR

Paul

GENRE

Epistle

PURPOSE

The book of Romans is arguably the greatest piece of theological literature for the Christian. It is dense and weighty in its expression of the gospel of Jesus Christ. Paul explains how the Old Testament laws and promises are fulfilled in the person and work of Jesus.

Because you have already read the Old Testament, much of Paul's allusions to it will make sense to you. But be prepared to jump back and refresh your mind on some other things that he refers to. You will need to take your time going through this book, which is full of theological language.

The purpose of the book of Romans is to show God's people how desperate their situation really is. It puts Jesus as the only hope for salvation. And it calls Jesus a gift given to us by God. Paul is absolutely convinced that we are saved by grace through faith alone. Paul calls his wonderful message the gospel, the power for salvation, for the Jew and gentile.

KEY VERSE

Romans 6:23

The Roman Road

SCRIPTURE READINGS

Day One: **2 Corinthians 1-4**
Day Two: **2 Corinthians 5-9**
Day Three: **2 Corinthians 10-13**
Day Four: **Acts 20:1-3; Romans 1-3**
Day Five: **Romans 4-7**
Day Six: **Romans 8-10**
Day Seven: **Romans 11-13**

SUMMARIES

Day One: **2 Corinthians 1-4**

In these chapters, Paul holds high the gospel of Jesus Christ. He is amazed that such a precious message would be contained in "jars of clay." We are just simple humans given the great responsibility and joy of sharing the most wonderful message in the world.

Day Two: **2 Corinthians 5-9**

We have the ministry of reconciliation, according to Paul. This means that it is our job to help other people understand that they are not in the right standing with God without Jesus. It also means that we are to help each other reconcile our relationships to one another as well.

Day Three: **2 Corinthians 10-13**

Sadly, there are some in the church who question Paul's ability to minister to them. They called into question his qualifications. And so, in these final chapters, Paul addresses some of the concerns that they have about him.

Day Four: Acts 20:1-3; Romans 1-3

The goal of the first three chapters in the book of Romans is to make it clear to the reader that they are sinners. This means they have broken the law of God and stand in his judgment. Paul leaves no escape for us when we think of our failure before God.

Day Five: Romans 4-7

After the harsh and difficult news of our sinfulness and failure before God, Paul gives us hope of the gospel. He explains that Jesus and his righteousness are given to us by faith in his death on the cross. Because of Jesus' sacrifice, we are now dead to sin and alive to God and him.

Day Six: Romans 8-10

The eighth chapter in Romans is called the greatest chapter in all of the Bible. It tells us that because of the work of Jesus, there is no condemnation for us. This means that we have no reason to feel guilty because Jesus has already paid for all of the sin and shame. It shows us that absolutely nothing will separate us from the love of God in His Son.

Day Seven: Romans 11-13

The final chapters in the book of Romans are very practical. They explain that because of the good news of the gospel, we are to live a different life than we did before. Paul says that our lives are like a sacrifice. That sacrificial life is our worship of God.

1. Do you agree with Paul that we are just jars of clay?

2. What does the Ministry of Reconciliation mean to you?

3. Do Paul's accusers have any right to question his ministry?

4. Are you convinced that you are a sinner?

5. Why do we need Jesus' righteousness for our own?

6. What does it mean that through one man, sin entered into the world, and through one man, life was given?

7. What of the practical commands at the end of the book of Romans is difficult for you to follow?

Colossians

AUTHOR

Paul

GENRE

Epistle

PURPOSE

The book of Colossians, like many of Paul's writings, can be split into two distinct portions. The first portion is a theological treatise. It presents Jesus as God himself. And because of who Jesus is, that directly affects how we are to live our lives.

In light of the truth of Jesus, as Lord, Paul tells the Christians in the church class to put off the old self and put on a new life in Christ. He goes into many examples of what that might look like. He includes things like how you should work, how you should treat others, and even how you should communicate with those around you.

The purpose of the book of Colossians is to correct and warn believers of the dangers of misunderstandings surrounding who Jesus is. However, if the church gets these foundational things right, then God will do mighty things through it.

KEY VERSE

Colossians 3:12-13

AUTHOR

Paul

GENRE

Epistle

PURPOSE

The book of Philemon is a different kind of letter. It is not a letter written to a church. It is a letter written to an individual who is a slave owner. Philemon had a slave named Onesimus. Onesimus robbed his master and ran away. Over the course of his journey, he became a Christian. Paul wrote this letter to set things right.

As Paul has gotten to know Onesimus, he has realized the genuineness of his faith. He calls Philemon to recognize that an SMS is no longer just a slave. Onesimus is a brother in Christ. And so Paul encourages him to treat him like he would a brother. He urged him to offer forgiveness and give a chance for repentance.

The purpose of the book of Philemon is to show that the gospel is not just a theological concept. It has everyday applications. It means that we have to forgive people that are hard to forgive. It means that we have to offer love and compassion to those who have hurt or wronged us. In short, it means that we have to live like Jesus. And that can be a very difficult thing to do at times.

KEY VERSE

Philemon 16

Ephesians

AUTHOR

Paul

GENRE

Epistle

PURPOSE

The book of Ephesians is one of my favorite books in the entire Bible. The opening chapter is an incredible display of how the fullness of God was involved in our salvation. The Father sat us. The sun bought us. And the Holy Spirit opened our eyes so that we could see the gift of grace.

This message so captivates Paul that he does not move on from it. In the second chapter, he continues to explain that we were once dead in our sins. But the mercy of God and the love he had for us has made us alive in Christ Jesus. And just like in his other letters, this means that our lives should look different after knowing Jesus.

The purpose of the book of Ephesians is to explain how the gospel breaks down the dividing walls that exist between people within the church. It explains how husbands are to love their wives like Christ loved the church. It explains how parents ought to raise their children with fear of the Lord in mind. There is so much to enjoy in this powerful book.

KEY VERSE

Ephesians 2:8

AUTHOR

Paul

GENRE

Epistle

PURPOSE

The book of Philippians is known by many as the book of joy. Paul begins with his overwhelming thankfulness for the faith that exists in the church in Philippi. He prays as God for how he has worked among them and how they have never failed to partner with him in the gospel.

One of the key ideas that is found in the book is humility. Paul looks to Jesus as his primary example of what humility truly looks like. It is almost as if he is saying that the key to joy in life is to put others before yourself. It is to hold them as more important than yourself so as to serve them like Jesus serves his people.

The purpose of the book of Philippians is to show believers that no matter what life circumstances are, there is a reason for joy. Paul writes this book while sitting in chains. He expresses in the letter that he has experienced poverty and wealth. And in all circumstances, he has learned how to be content because of what he knows through Christ Jesus.

KEY VERSE

Philippians 3:7

Paul's Final Journey

SCRIPTURE READINGS

Day One: **Romans 14-16**
Day Two: **Acts 20:4-38; Acts 21; Acts 22; Acts 23:1-35**
Day Three: **Acts 24-26**
Day Four: **Acts 27-28**
Day Five: **Colossians 1-4; Philemon**
Day Six: **Ephesians 1-6**
Day Seven: **Philippians 1-4**

SUMMARIES

Day One: **Romans 14-16**

Paul ends this letter in a similar way to how he started it. In the beginning, he says that the gospel is the power of salvation to all mankind. And now, in the end, he is holding up Jesus as the only hope for anyone who seeks to be saved.

Day Two: **Acts 20:4-23:35**

The end of Paul's ministry is a wild ride. He has direct conversations with God. He sees men rise from the dead. He is thrown into jail. There's not much more that Paul can experience on the missionary journey.

Day Three: **Acts 24-26**

Just like his Savior, Paul is put on trial. And just like His Savior, he is wrongfully accused of many things. Paul is a good speaker and brings a valuable defense to his faith and his actions before the various rulers.

Day Four: **Acts 27-28**

One of Paul's main goals in his missionary journeys was to finally make it to Rome. Finally, he has reached the point where he gets to go to Rome and stand trial. On his way, there are storms and shipwrecks. But even through all of the issues, Paul finally reaches his grand destination.

Day Five: **Colossians 1-4; Philemon**

If I can give you any encouragement today, I would encourage you to spend plenty of time in the first chapter of Colossians. There, you will find Paul's explanation of the deity of Christ. Soak those words in and let them amaze you at what God has done through his son.

Day Six: **Ephesians 1-6**

Understanding this book is a key to the Christian life. It makes it clear that we are in desperate need of the grace of God not only in our salvation but in our daily lives as well. We were once dead, and our sins are now alive because of Jesus. And the only thing that keeps us on the right track is Jesus himself.

Day Seven: **Philippians 1-4**

The book of Philippians is a Goodwin to read if you are struggling to find the joy in life. Paul makes much mention of Christian contentment. He says that in all circumstances he has faced, he has learned to be content through his faith in Jesus.

1. Why does Paul say that Jesus is the only hope for all of mankind?

2. Do you think you would have endured the trials that Paul went through on his journey?

3. What stood out to you about Paul's trial?

4. Why do you think Paul wanted to go to Rome?

5. How would you have handled the situation with Philemon and Onesimus?

6. What did you learn about the grace of God in the book of Ephesians?

7. In what areas of your life can you learn to be more content?

AUTHOR

Paul

GENRE

Epistle

PURPOSE

The book of First Timothy is a letter from a mentor to a mentee. Or, to put it as Paul phrases it, it is a letter from a spiritual father to a spiritual son. Paul has a deep love for Timothy and desires to train him as a pastor. Much of what Paul has to share with Timothée in this letter is practical advice for the Ministry.

Paul explains to Timothy how men and women are to behave in the church. He goes over it with the qualifications for pastors and for deacons. He even goes on to explain how the church ought to care for widows that exist within the congregation. Paul leaves no stone unturned when giving advice to his beloved, spiritual son.

The purpose of the book of First Timothy is to give a blueprint for how the church is to be managed. It describes and defines the two offices that exist within the church: the pastor and the Deacon. It explains how men and women ought to worship together and work together in the midst of the church.

KEY VERSE

1 Timothy 3:15

Titus

AUTHOR

Paul

GENRE

Epistle

PURPOSE

The book of Titus is another letter from a mentor to a mentee. Paul's relationship is not as close to Titus as it is to Timothy. But he still has plenty of advice to give his brother.

Titus was the pastor of the church in Crete that Paul had planted. However, this church struggled to gain momentum. And so Paul is sending a letter to encourage and instruct Titus on how to move forward. One of the key things that he expresses to Titus is to a Point and raise up elders or pastors in the church. Without the proper leadership, it has very little chance of being successful. The qualifications for a Pastor are reiterated in short in this book.

The purpose of the book of Titus is to re-emphasize the importance of the pastor's role in the life of the church. Paul spins plenty of Inc. speaking to pastors and encouraging them to lead in a godly manner. In two of the three pastoral epistles, the qualifications for a pastor can be found. Paul takes this office very seriously, and so should the church today.

KEY VERSE

Titus 1:5

AUTHOR

Peter

GENRE

Epistle

PURPOSE

The book of First Peter is a letter written to persecuted and struggling churches and Christians. Peter does not shy away from nor downplay the seriousness of the persecution that they are facing. Rather, he puts forth the hope that we have in Jesus and the comfort of the heavenly home that awaits us as fuel to the fire of the believer.

One of the interesting points that Peter makes is that the Christian arts rejoice in the sufferings that they endure because, in them, they share the sufferings of Christ. Peter counted it an honor to be persecuted for the name of his savior, and he encouraged the church to count it as an honor as well.

The purpose of the book of First Peter is to encourage the Christian who is enduring suffering and persecution for the sake of Christ. Peter makes it clear, though, that simple suffering is not what he's talking about. He is specifically speaking about suffering in the name of Jesus. And in that suffering, he tells the church to be able to express the hope they have in Him.

KEY VERSE

1 Peter 2:9

Hebrews

Unknown

Epistle

PURPOSE

The book of Hebrews is an incredible work of the Ology. Although we do not know the author, whoever it was was brilliant. He essentially takes the entire Old Testament and shows how Jesus is the answer to it all. There is a motif of Jesus being the greater version of the one that was before him that goes the whole way.

The author of the book of Hebrews explains that Jesus is the greater Moses and the greater David. He shows how Jesus is the better temple and the more excellent sacrifice. He goes to great lengths to explain how Jesus fulfills the entire Levitical system. Because of this book, we know much more about the purpose of the Old Testament.

The purpose of the book of Hebrews is simply to say that Jesus is greater. Whatever hero of the faith that exists in the Old Testament pales in comparison to him. While we are thankful for those brothers and sisters and can learn a lot from them, the author and perfectionist of our faith still remains Jesus Christ alone.

KEY VERSE

Hebrews 12:1-2

AUTHOR

Paul

GENRE

Epistle

PURPOSE

The book of second Timothy is a special one because it is essentially the last recorded words of Paul. As he is imprisoned in Rome and awaiting his execution, he sends this letter to his dear brother Timothy. The emphasis of the letter is on the word of God.

He tells Timothy that all scripture is breathed out from God. This means that all of scripture is God's word. He also encourages Timothy to preach the word. He makes sure that Timothy is not drawn into the drama and gossip of the local church, but he sticks to the one thing he knows to be true. Just as Paul has been a mentor to Timothy, and he encourages Timothy to set an example to all of the believers in his church. There is no doubt that Timothy is expected to have taken on a minty of his own.

The purpose of the book of a second Timothy is to encourage those who are in ministry to persevere in the faith and to proclaim the gospel at all costs. It can be easy for pastors and those who are serving in ministry to get sidetracked on all kinds of topics. But the one topic that is never worth leaving is the good news of Jesus.

KEY VERSE

2 Timothy 3:16-17

Pastoral Letters

SCRIPTURE READINGS

Day One: **1 Timothy 1-6**
Day Two: **Titus 1-3**
Day Three: **1 Peter 1-5**
Day Four: **Hebrews 1-6**
Day Five: **Hebrews 7-10**
Day Six: **Hebrews 11-13**
Day Seven: **2 Timothy 1-4**

SUMMARIES

Day One: **1 Timothy 1-6**

Paul writes many letters to the pastors that he has trained. The letter to Timothy explains what the church ought to look like. He lays out for Timothy different offices to do and who is qualified to hold them.

Day Two: **Titus 1-3**

Paul's letter to his brother in the ministry, Titus, is one full of encouragement. He expresses the importance of raising and equipping qualified pastors. He pushes Titus forward in the difficult work that he has ahead of him.

Day Three: **1 Peter 1-5**

This letter from Peter is for the persecuted and suffering Christians. As you read the words that he has to say, you will see his unwavering hope for the future life of the Christian. The unfading and untarnished joy of heaven is what keeps Peter going.

Day Four: **Hebrews 1-6**

The opening chapter of his book is the key to understanding it all. The author of Hebrews says that Jesus is the highest of all things. He is higher than us and greater than the angels. He is the expressed image of God himself.

Day Five: **Hebrews 7-10**

In these chapters, the author of this book makes it clear that Jesus is the greatest version of anything we have ever seen. Whether it is a Priest, prophet, or King, Jesus is the greater version of them all. Even down to the Levitical system in the sacrifices involved, he is the greater sacrifice.

Day Six: **Hebrews 11-13**

The 11th chapter contains many people called the Hall of Faith. All of the great heroes of the Old Testament and their faith are explained and highlighted. And in the midst of it all, it is sad that Jesus is both the author and perfecter of their faith and ours. Because that is his role, we can just drive to have faith like our forefathers.

Day Seven: **2 Timothy 1-4**

The second letter to Timothy, or Paul's final words to his dear brother. He encourages him to preach the word of God and that alone. He tells him that, although he is young, he is still able to set an example of godliness for the people that are in his congregation. Just like Paul was to him, he encourages Timothy to find someone to pour into.

1. Why is a proper order to church leadership so important to Paul?

2. Why does Paul tell Titus to raise pastors in order to help his church?

3. Have you ever faced persecution for your faith?

4. What answer would you give for the hope that is in you?

5. In what ways is Jesus the greater prophet?

6. How can Jesus be a once and for all sacrifice?

7. Who in the hall of faith is one of your heroes?

Peter and Jude

Epistle

The messages of 2 Peter and Jude are so similar that it is worth putting them together in this introduction. Although they are written by two completely different authors, their focus is the same. There are false teachers who are persecuting the church, and both Peter and Jude call their respective churches to contend for the faith.

Peter encourages the Christians to know the word so well that they can contend for the faith no matter who is in front of them. Jude tells the believers that he is communicating the seriousness of the situation that the false teachers find themselves in. Both Peter and Jude make it plain that false teachers will be charged for the work that they are doing. God will not overlook those who are trying to disrupt and divide his church.

The purposes of Jude and 2 Peter are basically the same. Both authors want their churches to fight for doctrinal purity. They make it clear that what we believe about the word of God really matters. And they also make it plain that anyone who disrupts the church by spreading falsehood about what the church believes will be punished by God himself.

2 Peter 3:9; Jude 3

1 John

John

Epistle

PURPOSE

The gospel, according to John, is to convince the reader that Jesus is God. The letter of First John is to remind and encourage the Christians that their faith is indeed genuine. He writes much of what he has to write to let Christians know whether or not their faith in Jesus is real.

He gives practical examples along the way to be a litmus test for authentic faith. He uses phrases like the light cannot be with the darkness. He makes the statement that living in sin is incompatible with the Christian faith. His letter is like the book of James in that way, but it comes with a more theologically driven tone. The purpose of the book

The purpose of the book of First John is to encourage the believer to abide in Christ. It is through abiding in him that we are saved. And it is through abiding in him that we can be confident of our salvation each and every day. That is the one test that must be passed by any believer that they abide in Jesus by their faith.

KEY VERSE

1 John 5:13

AUTHOR

John

GENRE

Epistle

PURPOSE

In the second book of Second John, John fights against the false doctrines that have spread around Jesus. There are some who are teaching that Jesus did not actually come in the flesh. These teachers hold to the idea that anything physical is evil. They would say anything spiritual is good. Therefore, they believe that if he had had a physical body, he would have been evil. And so they tease that he was just a spirit.

John pushes back against this erroneous teaching. Jesus took on the flesh. That was key to the mission that he set out to accomplish. Without the share the blood of Christ, there would be no forgiveness of sins. Without a physical body, he would've had no need to eat nor an ability to weep. But he did both of those things and bore our sins on the cross in the flash.

The purpose of the book of Second John is to encourage believers to express their love and trust in Jesus by obeying his commands. Because Jesus lived in a physical body, and God works in that body. He encourages believers to do the same.

KEY VERSE

2 John 6

3 John

John

Epistle

PURPOSE

The Book of Third John is a short and powerful book. John holds no punches, and he speaks to some of the members of the church that he is communicating with. He has three people in mind, and he has things that need to be sad.

The first is to his beloved brother in the gospel, Gaius. He encourages him to show hospitality to those who are coming through his city and preaching the same gospel that he is. Secondly, he speaks to die trophies. Diatrophies is a poor leader in the church that is causing all kinds of issues. Finally, he addresses, by name, Demetrius. He encourages them to look at the example that Demetrius has set and follow it.

The purpose of the Book of Third John is to speak to the leaders of the church in Ephesus and encourage where needed, and discipline were needed. We would learn a lot from the book of Third John if we were to take leadership in our churches seriously. When someone is doing well, applaud them. When someone is leading us astray, Stop them.

KEY VERSE

3 John 4

AUTHOR

John

GENRE

Epistle

PURPOSE

The Book of Revelation is an epic ending to the word of God. And I mean that literally. The sights and visions that John has while writing this book are of epic proportions. Like the visions found in the book of Daniel, they can be overwhelming to read and difficult to understand.

The key to understanding the Book of Revelation is actually found in the very first verse. This is a revelation of Jesus Christ. That means that it is not only from him, but it is about him. The whole point of the Book of Revelation is to explain how Jesus will return in power and glory. In dramatic fashion, it explains what the final war between God and the devil will look like. I don't want to spoil the ending, but God wins.

The purpose of the Book of Revelation is to show that while Jesus came humble, meek, and mild the first time, he would come back as a warrior. The king, his throne will never be overtaken, will begin his reign at his second coming. They promised Messiah, and that everyone was expecting the first time will now come in the end.

KEY VERSE

Revelation 19:11

An Epoch Ending

SCRIPTURE READINGS

Day One: **2 Peter 1-3; Jude**
Day Two: **1 John 1-5**
Day Three: **2 John; 3 John**
Day Four: **Revelation 1-5**
Day Five: **Revelation 6-11**
Day Six: **Revelation 12-18**
Day Seven: **Revelation 19-22**

SUMMARIES

Day One: **2 Peter 1-3; Jude**

These two letters are often read together. Although they have different authors, their message is the same. They provide a firm warning against false teachers. They not only tell the church that it is their responsibility to protect the truth, but they warn false teachers that it will be their demise if they continue to spread lies.

Day Two: **1 John 1-5**

If you have ever wondered if you are really a Christian, the letter that John writes here is for you. Many times throughout the letter, he makes the statement that he writes these things so that you may know. Take time to evaluate your faith as you read this book.

Day Three: **2 John; 3 John**

These final two letters of John are addressed to the elect lady and her children. There is some debate over who this person is and what it represents. I would encourage you to take the viewpoint that the elected lady is simply a godly woman who is a pillar of faith among the people in the church.

Day Four: **Revelation 1-5**

You have almost made it to the end of the Bible. Like many things, the best has been saved for last. John is giving a glimpse of the future in these pages, and he sees the end of the story. What you are about to read is supposed to be a great encouragement to you.

Day Five: **Revelation 6-11**

In these chapters, the difficult imagery begins to come. It can be hard to know what all of these symbols represent. Try not to get wrapped up in the guessing game. And look for Jesus along the way. He is the point of it all.

Day Six: **Revelation 12-18**

The great battle that is described in these chapters is of epic proportions. The enemy of God and the people of God in a great war. God's people are protected and kept safe, but the enemy is fierce. I can imagine that John was on the edge of his seat as the visions rolled in.

Day Seven: **Revelation 19-22**

Jesus wins. He is the rider on the Whitehorse. He is the husband who has made his bride, the church, Ready. He is the maker of the new heaven and new earth. He is the rightful king of the new Jerusalem. And he is the one who is coming soon. And so I say with the apostle John, "Come quickly, Lord Jesus!"

1. Why is it so important to remove false teachers from the church?

2. Do you ever doubt your salvation?

3. Which of the seven letters to the churches in Revelation stood out to you?

4. What did you learn about Jesus in the Book of Revelation?

5. Which of the images in the Book of Revelation was difficult for you to understand?

6. How did you feel as you read about the marriage between Jesus and the church?

7. Is there anything that keeps you from longing for Jesus' return?

When you set out on this adventure of reading the Bible in chronological order, I do not know where you were spiritually. However, I can promise that one thing is true today: you're not where you once were. As you have read, "So shall my word be that goes out from my mouth; it shall not return to me empty, but it shall accomplish that which I purpose, and shall succeed in the thing for which I sent it" (Isaiah 55:11, ESV). God's word has done work in your life by the power of the Spirit. And so now, I encourage you, do not slow down in your study. Dig into God's word through devotions, Christian books, and time in the Word. See what else the Lord has to teach you.